Tu Success!
A Journey from Pain to Purpose

A Memoir

Mariatu Tu Browne

Copyright © 2022 Mariatu Tu Browne

All rights reserved. No part of this book may be reproduced or used in any manner without the prior written permission of the copyright owner, except for the use of brief quotations in a book review.

To request permissions, contact the publisher at tu@tuorganics.com.

First paperback edition September 2022

Edited by Joan Stanford
Cover Photographer by Jessica King

Tu Organics LLC
10300 W Charleston Blvd Suite 17
Las Vegas, NV 89135

https://tuorganics.com

Dedicated to Beatrice Ella Hill, my mother. I don't remember you expressing or saying I love you too often. But I know you love me. You showed it to me through your actions. Your nurturing and support paved my way and gave me the confidence to keep striving for greatness. I love you.

"I am a Woman Phenomenally.
Phenomenal Woman, that's me."

- MAYA ANGELOU

Contents

Foreword ... 9
A Note from Tu ... 11
Prologue ... 13

Part 1 SIERRA LEONE, WEST AFRICA ... 17
Chapter 1 **A Man Named Murray Kallon** ... 19
Chapter 2 **The Mende Culture** ... 23
Chapter 3 **"Uncle" Fofanah** ... 29
Chapter 4 **A Buried Secret** ... 33
Just My Tu Sense (Lessons Learned) ... 38

Part 2 STATEN ISLAND, NEW YORK ... 39
Chapter 5 **Arriving in America** ... 41
Chapter 6 **Bobby and Solo** ... 45
Just My Tu Sense (Lessons Learned) ... 51

Part 3 ST. PAUL, MINNESOTA ... 53
Chapter 7 **On My Own** ... 55
Chapter 8 **Tutu** ... 59
Just My Tu Sense (Lessons Learned) ... 65

PART 4 **MILWAUKEE, WISCONSIN** 67

CHAPTER 9 **MOVING BACK HOME** 69

CHAPTER 10 **PERCY** 73

CHAPTER 11 **INTO THE FIRE** 83

CHAPTER 12 **MOM** 89

JUST MY TU SENSE (LESSONS LEARNED) 92

PART 5 **HAWTHORNE, CALIFORNIA** 93

CHAPTER 13 **A CLEAN SLATE** 95

CHAPTER 14 **KING HENRY VIII** 101

CHAPTER 15 **A NEW BEGINNING...AS A BUSINESS OWNER** 107

JUST MY TU SENSE (LESSON LEARNED) 111

PART 6 **INLAND EMPIRE** 113

CHAPTER 16 **LEAVING DANCING BEHIND** 115

CHAPTER 17 **BECOMING A WIFE** 125

CHAPTER 18 **FINDING GOD** 137

CHAPTER 19 **GETTING BACK UP** 139

CHAPTER 20 **OPHELIA** 143

CHAPTER 21 **MY GOLDEN TICKET** 147

CHAPTER 22 **CLOSED DOORS** 155

CHAPTER 23 **A TOUGH ROAD** 165

CHAPTER 24 **BECOMING PROFESSOR BROWNE** 169

CHAPTER 25 **SHINING DURING THE STRUGGLE** 175

JUST MY TU SENSE (LESSON LEARNED) 184

PART 7 **NEVADA**   **185**

CHAPTER 26 **YOU'RE GOING TO VEGAS!**   **187**

CHAPTER 27 **TU IN NEVADA**   **193**

EPILOGUE   195

THANK GOD   199

TU SUCCESS! A JOURNEY FROM PAIN TO PURPOSE BOOK RESOURCES: 200

ACKNOWLEDGEMENTS   203

Foreword

To him who overcomes I will grant to sit with Me on My throne, as I also overcame and sat down with My Father on His throne.

- Rev 3:21 NKJV

If I were to pick one word to describe Tu Browne it would be "Overcomer." When you read her life story you will be humbled by her persistence in meeting and overcoming every obstacle this world could throw at her. To be a successful small business owner I think you need the following: (1.) a dream or vision of what you want your business to look like, (2.) a single-minded determination to make that dream a reality, (3.) a strong constitution to withstand all the hurdles that will be thrown in front of you and (4.) a dedication to taking advantage of all the resources available through our education system, government programs, and community support agencies. I have known Tu for about seven years now. We met when I was her teacher in my entrepreneurship class she took at Cal State University in San Bernardino to earn her degree. From the beginning she had that vision of what she wanted. As I learned more about her, I have seen she exemplifies each of the characteristics I listed above. As you will see when you read her story, Tu demonstrates the best of what the American dream can offer – to those who are willing to reach for it. The odds were stacked against her. She was an immigrant. She suffered a personal bankruptcy. She faced many setbacks every step along the way. But she has made it. And you too, dear reader, can follow her example to find your personal business success. Today I still teach at the University, however the program Tu went through is now called the School of Entrepreneurship. The School is proud of its graduates and recognizes their success. Prominently displayed in the main seminar classroom are pictures of successful graduates. Among them is a 3' by 4' picture of Tu at her salon. She is one of the heroes of the School. She is one of my heroes, too.

Bill Donohoo

Professor of Entrepreneurship

A Note from Tu

I wrote this book in the hopes of inspiring and encouraging women who have endured domestic violence, molestation, and mental and verbal abuse. We must stop suppressing our pain to grow and blossom into our true selves. Reinventing myself was difficult and coming to terms with all my abuse was painful. The sacrifices and struggles were exhausting. But, I was determined to keep climbing. That is why I needed to invite God into my life. God's presence was around me, but I wanted to have a relationship with God, and once I did, I felt peace and hope and learned to forgive and feel forgiven. So, dear readers, some of you might be struggling, and maybe your personal life is in shambles. But keep going and get a relationship with God. God sees, and he adores us all.

Please note that this is a work of nonfiction. It is my story and my life as I remember it. All the events and experiences detailed on these pages are true and have been written as I recall them. Some names, identities, and circumstances have been changed in order to protect the privacy of the various individuals mentioned.

Conversations have been written as I remember them, but they have not been written to represent word-for word documentation. I've retold them in a way that evokes the feeling and meaning of what was said, keeping with the essence of the mood or spirit of the event.

Prologue

———•••◆•••———

On my first day at the Cheetah Club, I was scared as fuck! I was young, barely in my twenties, and had never danced in front of a room full of men before. I mean, I had gone out to nightclubs with friends and danced to the latest jams, but this was different. This was my first time at a strip club as a dancer and I was beyond nervous. Not to mention, the club was located on the Northside of Milwaukee, a high crime area, so anything could happen.

I was terrified and literally shaking in my thigh high boots. I had no professional dance experience and was unsure of myself. What if I got up there and had a bad case of stage fright? What if the men just looked at me or worst, booed me? *Dear God, what would my family think about what I was about to do?*

As I walked through the metal detector and into the hole-in-the-wall club, I was met with darkness and then the soft glow of red neon lights. The place smelled musty like old, wet carpet. Music was blasting from an old jukebox in the corner. I think it was Sir-Mix-a-Lot's "Baby Got Back." That song always had girls shaking their butts.

Several men of all different types were smoking cigarettes, drinking and calling out to the dancer on the makeshift stage. It was more like a platform that was about four feet off the ground. There were no stripper poles and no DJ, just that stage. So, dancers had to master dancing seductively, crawling on their knees and elbows and maintaining balance while wearing 8-inch platform heels. One false move and you could tumble off that stage and face plant onto that nasty floor.

You had old men in there who looked like they should be eating Jell-O at a nursing home. You also had the wannabe hip hop gangsters, and the business guys who you could tell worked in corporate America and were there to unwind while living a secret part of their lives.

As a rookie at the Cheetah Club, I had to observe closely and pick up on what the other dancers were doing and how they worked it. Of course, when it was my turn, I planned to add a little extra to it, if I could work up the nerve. It's funny because as I was watching and taking mental notes, the veteran dancers were staring me down too.

I looked like no other dancer in the place. I wore my hair in dreadlocks, which combined with my African features and body with curves in all the right places, gave me a distinctive, exotic look (at least that's what I was told). Plus, my dance outfit was more high-end sexy rather than hoochie. Percy (who I'll tell you about later) made sure I was dressed to impress in a diamond mesh lingerie top with the G-string to match. Compared to the other dancers I was bringing a class act to a ghetto ass club.

Finally, a bartender told me that I would be up next. I took a deep breath and slammed my fourth shot of Hennessey. It was time for me to show 'em what this rookie was working with. I ignored the knots in my stomach, pranced over to the jukebox and found the song I wanted. The beginning with the violins gave me a chance to strike my pose before rapper Juvenile started in with "Girl, you working with some ass yeah…" in Back That Thang Up. The club erupted and I was no longer nervous.

I licked my lips, bent over, and shook my hips in rapid-fire style. Oh, yeah, I was twerking before there was a name for it. I danced close enough to the edge of the stage so the men, whose jaws were dropped, could reach up and tip me. Some stuffed bills in my G-string while others tossed crumpled money onto the stage. If I wanted them to dig deeper into their wallets and make it rain, I knew I had to kick it up a notch. While down in a squatting position I flashed my goodies and the cash kept coming. I danced two more songs and was excited by the money and the power I seemed to possess. I'm not going to lie. It was intoxicating.

As I quickly glanced at the men closest to the stage, my eyes locked with one I hadn't noticed before. He was clearly African and the look on his face was a mixture of both shock and disgust. I forced an awkward smile, gathered the cash and made a mad dash for the exit.

You see, where I'm from—Sierra Leone in West Africa—women are held to a very high standard, and I had just been caught with my ass out. Literally!

PART 1
SIERRA LEONE, WEST AFRICA

Chapter 1
A Man Named Murray Kallon

"I cannot think of any need in childhood as strong as the need for a father's protection."

- SIGMUND FREUD

People think they know you, but honestly, they have no idea. Allow me to introduce myself and take you to the beginning of my journey, way before I started dancing for money and long before I became a college professor and a successful entrepreneur. My name is Mariatu Tu Browne, but everybody calls me Tu. I was born Mariatu Kallon in 1977. I'm the second of my mother's four daughters. Sarah is the oldest, then there's me, my sister Susan and the youngest is Ella.

I am the only one named after my grandmother, Mariatu Fofana of the Fofana family, a prominent, highly respected family in Bo, Sierra Leone. The Fofanas are not quite African royalty like in the movie *Coming to America*, but financially they're quite comfortable and well known by many. So naturally, the mere thought of a member of the Fofana family working as an exotic dancer in a United States strip club would be considered a total disgrace and an embarrassment to the family.

I grew up in a small community called Hanga Town in Bo, Sierra Leone. The town is within walking distance from the Bo Government

Secondary School. Bo School, as it's commonly known, was founded in 1906 and has a long history of developing the elite of Sierra Leone, especially the country's politicians. Think of it like an Ivy League high school where well-known public figures were groomed for excellence. Also in our local community were the government hospital, post office, police station, mosque, and shopping center. Everything we needed was nearby. Bo Town is the second-largest city in Sierra Leone after the capital, Freetown and the largest city in the country's southern province. But in Hanga Town, everybody knows everybody. If something happened, the rumors spread in a matter of minutes, not days or weeks.

As a member of the Fofana family, if you misbehaved word got back to my grandfather quick! He was a magistrate, which I've learned is like a lower level court judge. Back then I wasn't sure what his job was, but I knew the community looked up to him as a high ranking official. I recall an annual parade where my grandfather rode in front, waved at the people and was honored like a celebrity. My mom even has a photo of my grandfather sitting alongside the president back then. To the community he was this great man, but to me, he was the strict disciplinarian who had no problem beating my ass!

My grandmother, whom everyone called "Mama," was a chief's daughter. In our culture, a chief has multiple wives and children. Mama probably had close to one hundred siblings. She had no formal schooling, and in the ways of our tribe, she was married at a very young age to my grandfather, who was many years her senior. She was a housewife who raised her seven children and later her grandchildren.

She raised us as her own. We were well dressed, well fed, and attended the best Catholic schools in our community. Though we attended Catholic schools, my grandparents were Muslim, and we were raised Muslim.

My grandparents, my younger sister Susan, my cousins and myself.

One of those schools was an all-girls primary school called Queen of Rosary. Like all the schools in Sierra Leone, Queen of Rosary operated military-style. Nothing could be out of place, and I mean nothing! Everything was to be in order from your head to your toes, or you got severely disciplined by your teacher. Your parents (or grandparents) had no say in the school's choice to punish students.

Overall, I was a happy-go-lucky kid who loved to play and dance. And like any other child, I was disciplined if I did something wrong. Throughout my childhood in Africa, my sisters and I lacked nothing, except for maybe our parents' presence. Mom was off in Liberia chasing her entrepreneurial dreams and dad, well, that's a different story.

My siblings and I have different fathers. Their dad lived in a neighboring community, but mine lived in Kenema, which was nearly 40 miles away. It was so weird because while I knew he was my father, nobody confirmed for me that he was. It was almost like the identity of my father was an unspoken secret. He came around once in a blue moon and acted fatherly, but never said I was his daughter.

I have a vague memory of running away and going in search of my dad. I was probably around eleven years old, so I don't know how I managed to figure out what bus to take, but I hopped on a bus and found my way to his doorstep in Kenema. A woman, who I assume was his wife, answered the door. I stood there blankly at first and then mustered the courage to say, "I'm looking for Murray Kallon."

She looked me up and down said, "Who are you?"

"I think I'm his daughter."

My dad came to the door with worry in his eyes. He welcomed me into his home and was so concerned about me having traveled by myself. He fed me and later took me back to Bo.

Still, he never referred to me as his daughter. In fact, it wasn't until I was 30 years old and living in America that my mom somewhat confirmed that he was my dad.

She said, "Tu, I just wanted to let you know Murray died."

It was just like that, no emotion or anything. So based on her telling me he died, she basically confirmed what we all knew but never said… Murray Kallon was my father.

Upon hearing the news, I cried. I wailed like a baby because he was a father that I had, yet I didn't. During my childhood years I always felt a sense of abandonment and yearning for my father. And maybe, just maybe, his absence affected my future relationships with men. Yet, me not officially knowing him as my dad, I chalked it up to "that's just how they did things in my culture."

Chapter 2
The Mende Culture

---•••◆•••---

"We acquire the strength we have overcome."

- RALPH WALDO EMERSON

When I talk about my culture I'm referring to Mende (pronounced men-day). The Mende is one of the largest tribes or ethnic groups in Sierra Leone. Historically, most Mende people are farmers and hunters and live primarily in the southern part of the country, like in Bo where my family is from.

The Mende have traditional rituals and beliefs that have been passed down through the generations. For example, Mende people are true believers in initiating the young into adulthood through secret societies that are believed to hold power. So before the Mende children reach puberty, the initiation process begins for the boys "Poro" and the girls "Sande."

The goals of the Sande secret society are to teach young Mende women the responsibilities of adulthood. They taught us to be hardworking and modest in our behavior, especially toward our elders. Sande influences almost every aspect of a Mende woman's life, from how she styles her hair to who she marries.

A woman's hair is a sign of femininity in our culture. Both thickness and length are elements that the Mende people admire. Thickness means the woman has more individual strands of hair, while the length is proof of strength. It takes time, care, and patience to grow a beautiful full head of hair.

The Mende cultural ideas about a woman's hair connect to nature. The way the hair grows is compared to the way forests grow. A woman with long, thick hair illustrates a life force.

In addition, hairstyles are essential in Mende society. A Mende woman's hair has to be well groomed, clean, and oiled. Hair must be tied down under strict control and shaped into intricate, elegant styles for the sake of beauty and sex appeal. Dirty, messy hair is a sign of insanity. A woman who does not groom and maintain her hair has neglected the community's standards of behavior. Only a woman in mourning can let her hair loose. Mende finds unarranged, "wild" hair immoral and associates individuals with this trait with wild behavior. As a young girl with no dolls to play with, I braided my neighborhood friend's hair and had fun doing it. I think that was my early start to my hairstyling career.

Beyond hair, another important aspect of the Mende culture is its focus on gardening. It is considered a blessing for Mende women to possess a green thumb. They say it gives her the ability to have a promising farm and many healthy children. Although I am not into farming, anyone who visits my salon would attest to the beautiful plants there, validating my "green thumb."

A huge part of the culture and Sande initiation is undergoing a clitoridectomy (which is the surgical removal, reduction, or partial removal of the clitoris), also known as genital mutilation. This surgery is supposed to foreshadow the pain a Mende woman experiences during childbirth. The shock of this experience also tests a Mende woman's physical endurance. The shared pain of the clitoridectomy is supposed to create permanent bonds among the initiates. After the operation, you take vows that express a social bond; they are a metaphor for the women's support during the pains of childbirth.

This procedure they believe is necessary to change Mende children—considered to be of neutral sex before the process—into heterosexual, gendered adults. In addition, genital mutilation is said to remove the female's residue of maleness. My grandmother went through it, as did my mom, my siblings, and my cousins.

I was nine years old when I underwent the procedure. For me, it was one of the most traumatic experiences of my life. I was taken away out of town to a desolate area, out in the jungle that seemed to be the middle of nowhere. A few women (only women are allowed to attend) escorted me inside a large mud hut. My heart felt like it was pounding outside of my little chest as I was held down by an elder, a woman who was easily 300 pounds. With no anesthesia and no warning I was cut in my most private parts with a straight razor blade. I let out a blood curdling scream! To make matters worse, they mistakenly cut me differently, and it caused me excruciating pain and anguish. I hollered and I cried a lot. As a young Mende woman, you are not supposed to cry, but I bawled. I couldn't help it. It felt like my lower extremities were on fire and I was surely going to die.

I cried so much that one of the head women within the society brought a bucket and put it under me to fill it up with my tears. Now, you know, a bucket is enormous. So there was no way I was actually going to fill the bucket. But it was symbolic. This surgery represents coming into womanhood and it's supposed to be painful, but you're not supposed to cry. As far as they were concerned, crying was for babies, not a grown woman.

I remember my grandmother had to bribe the head woman in the community with food or a goat to forgive me for acting like a child and crying.

This clitoridectomy (Mende call it "Bundo") practice is something that has been going on for generations. I'm sure it continues to this day, which is why I have never taken my girls to Sierra Leone, nor do I have any intention to visit. My girls have asked about visiting, but I could never. I know how it is in my culture. My aunts would find a way to put my children through this same brutal practice. I don't want them to go through that. My children will never experience that type of traditional practice.

The Mende culture also revolves around polygamy, often practiced by men. Women are to respect and be obedient to their husbands. Younger wives are to respect older wives. Although my mom is a Mende woman, she was never accepting of the polygamy practice. She wanted to marry a man she loved.

Her first husband, whom she married at a very young age, had multiple women. Theirs was a traditional Muslim marriage. To my understanding, it was an arranged marriage because my grandparents cared for her husband. He came into my grandparents' care because he attended the boy's school as my grandfather and most other educated men in the community.

Since the school was minutes away from our grandparents' compound, most of the boys who attended sometimes would find themselves cared for by my grandfather. This was the case with my mother's first husband. My grandfather liked him and took him under his wing. He later arranged for the young man to marry my mother.

My mother's husband cheated on her multiple times. Not wanting to settle for that type of marriage, she left him but eventually returned after he asked for forgiveness. Also, she didn't want to bring shame to her family name. However, while still married, she met my father, Murray Kallon, and they conceived me. Again, she returned to her husband after my birth.

My sister, Susan, was born two years later. After her birth, my mother started traveling to Liberia for business and eventually settled there. She told me being there made sense because the country used the dollar currency, making business more profitable. I now understand I inherited my entrepreneurial spirit from my mother. She left us, her children, with our grandparents while she worked on securing products to sell, the beginnings of a retail business. She never forgot about us, though, supporting us from a distance by sending money to my grandparents for our upkeep. I once asked her if she missed us.

"Every day. But I had a reason, and that reason was to one day come back and get my children."

My mother would eventually have my sister, Ella, with another gentleman but that relationship was short lived. She met my stepfather, fell in love and married him. From Liberia, she moved to America where she became a certified nursing assistant (CNA) and started a "side hustle" as a businesswoman. She eventually brought my sisters, stepfather, and me to America.

As a single mom, I now know the hard work and sacrifice it takes to accomplish the goals we set for ourselves. In the end, my mom united our family here in America. She is truly my hero. Sometimes I just wish she had been in Sierra Leone when I was growing up, if for no other reason than to protect me.

My sister, from the left Sarah, Ella, Susan and myself

Chapter 3
"Uncle" Fofanah

◆

"Being betrayed is one of the most valuable lessons life can teach."
- SHAINA TWAIN

As a young girl, I didn't know I needed to be protected, especially from a so-called family member. I have tried over the years to suppress my painful childhood memories, as many of them are hard to talk about, even now. But this, this changed me forever. I was just a kid, but I was robbed of my innocence.

When my grandmother sent my younger sister Susan and me to "Uncle" Fofanah's house for a vacation, I was ten years old. I remember Susan and me being so excited to be leaving town and going to a village. We went to the farm and did things we usually didn't do, like get wood and fetch water. We were excited to experience all that. We loved our "aunt" and "uncle" before the incident when they visited our grandparent's house.

"Uncle" Fofanah had money. He was a respected pharmacist with a most loving wife. At this time, their sons were around three and five years old. They had a live-in housemaid—a teenager—who did most of the household cleaning and cared for the boys. On the surface, this man was a prominent man with a good wife, but in reality he was predator who he took advantage of young, innocent girls at night as they slept. He probably did the same thing to the housemaid; she was always so quiet and obedient.

I can't remember the exact day when it happened, but I know it was around at midnight when I was sound asleep. My sister shared a room with me. Uncle Fofanah's wife, children, and housemaid slept in the other rooms. I don't know how long he was in the room, but I turned in bed and felt his big hands between my legs. He inserted his fingers into my vagina. I was scared because it was dark, and I did not know what was happening until I opened my eyes. I started to scream, but he covered my mouth and whispered that no one would hear me or come to my rescue. This disgusting man I called "uncle"—whom my grandmother trusted enough to send my sister and me to his home—stole my innocence.

It destroyed me and left me feeling helpless. *Who do I turn to for help? Will they believe me? Does his wife know what her husband does when she is sleeping? How do I behave around his family now? Will my grandmother believe me?*

These questions kept replaying in my head.

I was sick the next day, the day after that, and throughout the rest of our stay with them. I also made sure I slept close to my sister and never left her side. After that, I didn't want to be at their house anymore. So our visit was cut short. I still can't remember how we got back, but I was thrilled to be with my grandmother.

But how could I tell her that the person she trusted had molested me? I was sad and very lonely because I was afraid no one would believe me. In Africa, older family members won't believe you when you tell them something like that, especially if the person doing the molesting is a respected figure in your community.

So, I told no one.

Every time he visited our grandparents' house, he would try to convince me to get closer to him, but this time around, I knew what he was capable of doing. I kept my distance and I made sure to sleep with my grandmother whenever he came around. With her, I knew I would be safe. I kept my secret to myself until I came to America.

Chapter 4
A Buried Secret

"There is no greater agony than bearing an untold story inside you."
- MAYA ANGELOU

It was hard being a good kid with that secret buried inside me. I became extremely rebellious and filled with attitude. The once innocent girl was gone. I did things a young African girl my age would not normally do. I was not listening or doing what I was told. I started talking back, which is unacceptable in African culture and incredibly disrespectful. And no one knew why I was acting up.

I just wanted my mom, but she was not around, nor was my father. I felt abandoned. Thinking that nobody cared, I started to steal from my aunt, who married into wealth, and I gave the money to my friends. We would buy junk food and waste the money in general. I was always at my friends' houses instead of mine.

As I became more destructive and rebellious, my grandfather became more abusive physically. To him, it was strong discipline. But, by American standards, it was straight-up abuse. He would send me to go and get the tool he used to whip me. Sometimes it was his belt. Other times it was a branch from a tree. Spankings became Kunta Kinte beatings as he would use whatever might leave a scar on my body. I still carry those scars on my body today.

Even with all the beatings, I continued to act out. The house help at my grandparents' house caught on to what I was doing, and they began to manipulate me to steal even more for them—which I did without remorse.

One time I took so much money from my aunt and got caught! Since physical discipline was not working, they tried something else---humiliation by my peers. They told everybody in our community, and at school all the kids sang songs, making fun of me. I was so embarrassed. It was like I was the village idiot. From that moment, I never stole again.

Years later, in America, I finally found the courage to tell my mom what had happened with Uncle Fofanah. She told me she wished I had told her back in Africa.

"I'm not sure what I would have done," my mom said. "But I would have been able to confront your molester."

Beyond that one statement, she pushed what happened to me under the rug. She didn't react the way I would have wanted her to respond. I expected her to be furious, but instead she was almost nonchalant. Deep down I felt like it was her fault. She left me and my sisters. As far as I was concerned, that monster we had to call "Uncle" ruined my life and I began to feel resentment toward my mother.

Back in Africa, my rebellious behavior continued until my grandfather was too sick to beat me. I was around eleven years old, when he became ill. I was happy he was sick. I know this is evil of me to say. He was ill for the longest time. No one knew what he had. Looking back now, it was probably cancer because he was a heavy chain-smoker. He smoked several packs of cigarettes a day while sitting on our porch and listening to the BBC news on his old radio. I remember his favorite cigarette brand was 555.

I hated my grandfather. I don't ever remember having love for that man, and I don't remember crying or grieving when he died. And let me tell you, it was not a beautiful death either. He was in great pain and suffered! And I was glad he did. I felt it was God's way of punishing him for constantly beating me so severely. There was no remorse in my heart for my late grandfather. I still feel the same way today.

After his passing, I was elated because there was no one else to abuse me. I was wrong. My mom's younger siblings became my next abusers, physically, verbally, and emotionally. My mother had six siblings; she is the fourth in line. The fifth sibling, my uncle, would beat me, usually right after smoking marijuana or getting drunk. While under the influence, I became his little punching bag.

My mom's younger sister was so mean to me. She would say things like: "You are the ugliest thing I've ever seen," and "You are so ugly." She would laugh and say that my mom left my siblings and me behind and was never to return for us. "No one is ever going to love your sisters and you," she would say. She seemed to target me the most and kept asking me, "Why are you so ugly?" That shattered me inside and killed my soul. My aunt single-handedly ruined my self-esteem. For years, I walked around believing that I was ugly.

I couldn't understand why she was so mean to her own sister's children. I used to wonder what we did wrong. Even as a grown woman, I can't seem to hate my sister's children the way my mom's sister hated the sight of my siblings and myself.

The abuse at the hands of my mother's family left me with anger and hatred in my heart for them. Over the years it became hatred associated with Sierra Leone and once I left, I vowed I would never go back, and I haven't. Years of mistreatment will do that to you. I was literally mistreated until my mother decided it was time for my younger sister, Susan, and me to join her in the United States, right after my grandmother passed.

My beloved grandmother went to be with the Lord on July 4, 1991, two days before I turned thirteen. That was a massive blow to me because my grandmother was everything to me. Even though part of me believes she was the indirect cause behind my sexual molestation, I still loved her. Her death was devastating, and the worst part of it all was I was not at home when she passed because they sent me to go get my aunt, who lived miles away. While I was walking the journey with the sun beating down on my face, my grandmother was taking her last breath. So my siblings and cousins surrounded her when she died, but I was not present. I have always felt like I missed out on her last blessings to her grandchildren. I'm sure she had some words of wisdom or prayers for me, her namesake, but I wasn't there to hear or receive them.

Her passing brought my mom back to Africa from America for her funeral. My mom did not arrive on time for the burial but made it for the forty-day mourning. It is a sign of respect for Muslims to bury a person immediately after they pass away. Forty days later, the community gathers for a day of mourning. During this celebration, the family traditionally kills a cow and makes a lot of food. They invite the community to come and pray together, eat together, and celebrate and acknowledge the person who died so they can have a passageway to their resting in peace. During this gathering, the *imam*, or religious leader, will recite from the Quran. The family will give to charity and do good deeds on behalf of the dead person.

I was thrilled about my mom's return because my younger sister and I knew she would take us back with her. *We were going to America!* Both our grandparents had passed on, and her sisters had families. So Susan and I prayed she wouldn't leave us with them. Even though our aunts started to act kindly to us in my mom's presence, we knew the truth and what they were capable of. The damage from years of abuse had been done.

Everyone was excited to see my mom, including me. I remember standing at the door, hiding behind my auntie's living room wall, watching her speak with her sisters. I stared at her in awe. This was my first time laying eyes on my mother after years of her being gone, and she looked absolutely beautiful. Although she was wearing African attire, she didn't have the traditional African look. She looked more like a glamourous American movie star. Her hair was honey blonde, and she was speaking proper English. She noticed me standing in the doorway, and she made a hand gesture to come to her. I shook my head *no*. I eventually walked over, just staring at her. She asked me to hug her, and I gave her the tightest hug. I didn't want to ever let go of her.

My mom completed everything she had to for my grandmother's forty-day burial ceremony. Then, she told my younger sister and me we were going to America, but not to let anyone in our community know, not even our close friends.

My mom had a fear of voodoo. She had taken my sister Sarah to the U.S. first because Sarah had a medical issue with her leg and people in our community said the reason for the issue was voodoo that was intended for my mom. At this point, my mom was not taking any chances. She wanted to take Susan and I without any possible harm. So we did as she said and kept our leaving a secret.

I can't remember whether it was a couple of days or weeks, but we traveled from Bo Town to the capital of Sierra Leone and from there, to the United States.

Coming to America - Lungi Airport Freetown, Sierra Leone.

Just My Tu Sense
(Lessons Learned)

---◆---

It's okay to cry. Although I was raised to be a strong Mende woman who endures pain, almost as a badge of honor, I have learned that it is okay to feel emotions and it is perfectly normal to cry.

If you are ever forced into an uncomfortable position or you are touched inappropriately or sexually violated by anyone, please speak up and tell somebody about it. It is NOT your fault.

No matter what you are told or what you experience, you are a beautiful human being and you are loved.

PART 2
STATEN ISLAND, NEW YORK

CHAPTER 5
ARRIVING IN AMERICA

———•◆•———

"Offering yourself forgiveness and compassion for what has happened will help you let go of the past so that you can move more fully into the future."

- ALISON CARDY

In the fall of 1990, Susan and I touched down on United States soil with my mom and it was a blessing because civil war erupted in Sierra Leone in early 1991. If you watched the movie *Blood Diamond*, you have a sense of the calamity that was happening. It was an armed conflict that went on for 11 years and over 50,000 people lost their lives. So we got out of there just in time.

We also arrived in America just in time for school. My mom enrolled Susan and me at Edwin Markham Intermediate School 51 in Staten Island. Unfortunately, the school held me back a grade level and had us take an English-as-a-Second-Language (ESL) class.

While I was excited about being in America, middle school was not enjoyable for me at all. I was constantly picked on, made fun of and bullied. But interestingly, the class of 1992 voted me "Most Likely to Succeed" in the yearbook. For a girl just arriving from Africa, it meant nothing to me because I didn't understand the meaning behind it.

In September 1992, I started high school. My sister Susan and I had been inseparable until then. But, unfortunately, she was a grade behind me. So, my mom enrolled me at Ralph McKee Vocational Technical School. During this time, my mother moved us from the single-family house to a duplex on Faber Street because my sister Ella and stepfather were coming from Africa, and we needed a bigger space.

My stepfather and Ella had remained in Liberia when my mom left for the United States. Unfortunately, they were there when civil war broke out in that country. People were dying. But she managed to find a way to bring them to America before a tragic ending occurred. I don't know how my mother got all of us out of Africa on a CNA's paycheck, but she did. My mom had a live-in job caring for elderly people while my stepdad had a plumbing job. Every Sunday, my mom would come home to cook spaghetti and meatballs, and the entire family would be home. She took this Sunday meal idea from the Italian family she worked for.

We eventually all moved to the Park Hill Projects. Everybody called Park Hill Projects "Little Africa" because when Africans immigrated to the U.S. and settled in Staten Island, New York, they undoubtedly would live in Park Hill. Africans outnumbered the other nationalities who called Park Hill home. This subsidized housing building was the worst. It was roach- and rat-infested, with hallways and elevators that smelled like urine. The elevators were always breaking down. Oh, and on any given day, you would hear gunfire. Sadly, shootings in or around Park Hill were a way of life, so you weren't particularly scared. Instead, you wondered who was shooting or if you knew the victim who caught the bullets. Usually, it was the African gang members against the black American gang members.

You might be asking why in the heck would we live there, especially in a one-bedroom apartment. It's simple, actually. Our place in Park Hill was a low-income apartment, so the rent was super affordable. With my mom and stepdad both having jobs where they lived with their employers, my sisters and I had the apartment all to ourselves until we started moving out and going our separate ways.

One of my fondest memories is of our last Christmas together as a family in Park Hill; it was magical. I must have been sixteen. Our Christmas tree was about six feet tall, and we had so many gifts under it. I remember dressing up as Santa, and my sisters sat on my lap before handing them their gifts. It was the best Christmas ever for me.

Before I graduated from Ralph McKee Vocational Technical School, my stepdad taught me how to drive and I got my driver's license at age sixteen. My mom gave me a 1992 Honda Civic. She gave each of her daughters a car either before or after graduating high school. The only one who didn't receive one was Ella. She wanted nothing to do with school, so I guess my mom decided she didn't deserve a car.

But me, I excelled in all my classes, so I started my senior year going to school in my new car. While I was a good, responsible student, I was the dumbest girl when it came to acting responsibly with my vehicle. I kept getting parking tickets weekly because I parked any and everywhere without checking for "NO PARKING" signs. Whenever I got a parking ticket, I threw it in the glove compartment without thinking of the consequences.

By the time I graduated high school in June of 1996, I had racked up hundreds, maybe thousands, of dollars' worth in parking tickets without my mom's knowledge. After graduation, I was accepted into the College of Staten Island. I believe I attended the Fall 1996 semester, then dropped out at the end of that session, which greatly upset my mother. Her attitude towards me completely changed. Before dropping out, however, I had received Discover and Visa credit cards. I felt like I was on top of the world, and I became even more irresponsible.

During this time, Sarah had moved out while Susan graduated from high school and moved to Wisconsin for college. With my parents gone most of the time, Ella would come and go as she pleased. The apartment was basically mine. We were forced to grow up fast. My life would go from being voted as "Most Likely to Succeed" in junior high and high school to losing myself. And the downward spiral started with boys and dating.

Chapter 6
Bobby and Solo

"It takes great bravery to love someone, but even more courage to walk away when it's no longer right."

- UNKNOWN

Bobby was my first boyfriend, my first love, and my first experience with domestic violence. I was sixteen when we met. We lived across the street from each other in the Park Hill Projects. His family came from Liberia and lived in a two-bedroom apartment. I became friends with his stepsister and that was how we met. He was a clean-cut, nice guy who kind of resembled the R&B singer Usher. To me, he was fine! We saw each other every day. While I attended McKee, he went to Curtis High School, which was down the street. Bobby and I were inseparable. I was always at his house or he was at mine. We were constantly with each other after school or work (I had a job at McDonald's—my first job in America).

Everyone that was African at Park Hill knew us as a couple. What they didn't know was that Bobby was jealous and controlling. My first experience with his jealousy was him telling me what to wear. According to him, I should not wear dresses or skirts that overexposed my body. I began to dress the way he wanted me to just to please him. I even chose a prom dress I knew he'd approve of. It was silver with spaghetti straps and slit on the right side.

Since I was a year ahead of him in school, we went to my prom first. It was the worst experience of my high school days. I felt like I couldn't breathe. He didn't want me to dance with my classmates or leave our table without him by my side. He did allow me to dance with my female classmates, though. He watched closely to whom I spoke when on the dance floor.

At one point I stormed off the dance floor and got right up into his face. "This is crazy. Prom is supposed to be fun and I'm not having any fun because of you."

He shrugged. "Well, we can just leave then."

I expected him to apologize or tell me that he'd do better. But he had the nerve to say we could leave!

I was fed up. "Fine. Let's go!"

We left the prom super early and all I kept thinking was, *You just wait. Your prom is coming up and I will NOT be going with you.*

This whole prom incident should have been a red flag, but I thought nothing of it because I had convinced myself that he loved me. But then the emotional abuse turned into physical abuse.

I remember one hot summer day, I was wearing a short jean skirt and a tank top. Back then I was skinny with long legs. People would ask why I was not modeling. Shoot, I was too insecure for that. But on this day my insecurities went out the window because I had a boyfriend and he adored me. We were wildly crazy about each other. I went to watch him play soccer at the park. Afterward we were heading to my apartment and as usual in the projects, the elevator was broken. So we were forced to take the stairs. Almost as soon as we entered the stairwell, Bobby's handsome face became stone cold and he slapped the living daylight out of me. The force and hot sting of the slap felt like fire.

"Didn't I tell you not to wear revealing clothes like that?" He growled. Before I could respond, whap! I was met with another slap. This one harder than the first, powerful enough to leave the imprint of his hand on my cheek. I was shocked and tears streamed down my face. That was the first time Bobby hit me. Right then and there I told him I didn't want to be with him anymore. He immediately started apologizing and saying he would never do that again. Before I knew it, we were both crying and I forgave him because, well, I loved him. Remember, we were teenagers and he was my first love.

Bobby's insecurities and temper were out of this world. I would end up forgiving him over and over again. Mom liked Bobby for me, but she didn't know the abuse I was enduring by his hands. None of my family members knew. All they saw was the good boy image Bobby displayed. A year or so after the physical abuse started, I finally told Bobby it was over between us and I meant it that time. He kept apologizing, but I finally shouted, "I don't love you anymore. I love Solo!"

Shadrach, whom I called Solo, and Bobby were soccer teammates. Like Bobby, Solo was Liberian and lived at Park Hill. But Solo had a girlfriend who had recently given birth to his child. While Bobby had the reputation of being a squeaky-clean good guy, Solo was known as a bad boy. But he was a sexy bad boy. He had smooth chocolate skin and beautiful white teeth. He was like a short Idris Elba with dreadlocks. Once I started spending time with Solo, he introduced me to marijuana, cigarettes, and alcohol.

One day, I was with Solo at his apartment when Bobby came knocking at his door. Bobby discovered I was with Solo when he saw my gold Honda Civic parked in front of his apartment building. He came upstairs and banged on Solo's door, saying, "I know she's in there."

I was with Solo, smoking, drinking and having a good time. Although Bobby and I were over—at least that was what I thought—I still jumped out of the window and climbed down the fire escape, got into my car, and sped home. Solo later told me he invited Bobby into his apartment to look around for me, and since I was gone, Bobby left and went directly to my apartment. He could tell I was high, and I smelled like cigarettes. This time around, I made it clear.

"Bobby, you know our relationship has been over a long time ago. So why are you acting like we're together?" I slurred.

"Just answer me this. Why would you choose Solo over me?"

"You want to know why? Because he does not put his hands on me."

That night, Bobby did not leave my apartment. He spent the night apologizing endlessly and asking for me to reconsider my decision, especially now that his prom was approaching and he wanted me to be his date. I told Bobby I'd go with him but only if we went our separate ways after the dance. He agreed, and I let him hold me. We slept together on the living room floor that night, with both of us crying ourselves to sleep.

Since I had not planned on attending his prom, I didn't have a dress. A girlfriend of one of his brothers gave me one of her dresses and shoes. Bobby was on his best behavior at his prom. Unlike at my prom, we had a great time. After the dance, we spent one last night together, and in the morning, he went home, and that was the end of my first love.

Unlike Bobby, Solo was older than me and a high school dropout. But I wanted Solo at all costs, and since I had a car and credit cards, I bought the drinks and the smokes. Now that I look back, Solo didn't want me, but he liked what I could give him because I was buying his affection. Little did I know that he would be even more abusive than Bobby, but I had no clue in the beginning.

Solo's girlfriend and the mother of his daughter was Liberian too and a church girl, which made him very protective of her and her feelings. He didn't want her to find out about us. But Bobby made sure she knew. One day while I was at work doing security in a Park Hill building, I was sitting behind the counter with my walkie-talkie on my hip. I saw Solo's baby mama and her friend come in but paid the baby mama no attention. Instead, I chit-chatted with her friend, who I guess was there to distract me. Before I knew it, Solo's baby mama was behind and she smacked the hell out of me. I must have blacked out for a minute because suddenly the phone was ringing and the girls were gone. When I answered the phone it was my employer saying they saw everything that happened on the video camera and they were sending someone to relieve me. When that person arrived I went and filed a report and then rushed home to change out of my uniform. It was on!

I called my cousins and told them what happened and they were ready to ride. "Let's go find her," they said.

We headed for Solo's apartment, where I knew she'd go. I banged on the door, yelling "Let her come out. I know she's in there and I'm going to beat her ass!"

He screamed back through the door, "If you touch her, I'm going to beat YOU!"

"Whatever. It's on!" I said.

I left with my cousins and we went to the park to bide our time. The park was where everybody hung out. Kids played, adults drank and smoked. People were out selling a variety of African foods and other items like roasted corn. My cousins went to play handball, but I just stood there, heated. About an hour or so later, I caught a glimpse of Solo's baby mama. She strolled out of the apartment building without a care in the world.

Before I could tell my cousins, I rushed that girl so fast, picked her up and slammed her. I proceeded to beat her like I was Mike Tyson, throwing punches back-to-back. She was bruised and bleeding before they pulled me off of her.

Of course, Solo's friends ran to go tell him what happened. True to his word, Solo beat me up and that was the first time I experienced his abuse. Afterward he said he didn't want anything to do with me. Silly me, I begged and apologized. I didn't want him to leave me. I thought I was in love. He kept ignoring me, though.

Finally, I got a clue and decided not to give him any more attention. I started going out to clubs with my friends and doing my own thing. His friends that knew about us would go back and tell him they saw me in a club dancing with some other guy. Solo would show up at my place in a jealous rage. I was confused. He had said he wanted nothing to do with me, yet he acted crazy at the thought of me with other guys. Solo and I would make up and break up; I would find myself begging him to take me back after every breakup. It was all so stupid, reflecting back on it. Solo was a toxic person and no good for me.

Here I was, nineteen years old, and I had gone from being an excellent student to a stoner and drinker. Because Solo was selling weed, we had an endless supply, so we always smoked. I got to the point where I woke up in the morning and immediately rolled a blunt. It was a horrible downward spiral.

Then things got worse when I had it out with my mom. She found out about all the parking tickets and my drinking and smoking habits.

"You're not the daughter I brought from Africa," she said.

"Well, you're not the mother I thought you were!" I fired back.

She just shook her head with disgust. "I'm taking your car. You don't deserve it."

"If you take my car, I'm leaving New York and not coming back."

"Go!"

True to her word, she took away my car and sold it to pay for my parking tickets, and my license got suspended. With no license and no car, I decided to leave New York for Minnesota.

Just My Tu Sense
(Lessons Learned)

Be a leader, not a follower.

Love is a two-way street, a mutual experience. If you "love" someone, you should see and feel their love as well. A man who hits you doesn't love you.

Your living arrangements or environment do not define you. You can live in the hood, be raised in the projects, and still make a good life for yourself.

If you're a teenager or young adult, you have a lot to learn. No matter how much you THINK you know, you don't know so many things. Be open to learning and focus on making good decisions.

PART 3
ST. PAUL, MINNESOTA

Chapter 7
On My Own

"Change and growth can be tough. But nothing is as tough as staying stuck in the same place where you aren't meant to be."

- LEWIS HOWES

For the life of me, I still can't remember how I got to Minnesota. But I know it was not by plane because I was scared of flying, and even if I weren't afraid, I wouldn't have been able to afford a plane ticket.

Nevertheless, I arrived in Minnesota in the summer of 1997 with a small suitcase, my suspended driver's license, Social Security card, and green card. I chose Minnesota because a friend told me there were good-paying jobs there. So, I stayed with a close friend's uncle and his family. A week later, after arriving, I made a new friend with a young lady named Jennifer. She was very familiar with the Minnesota housing system because she lived in low-income housing with her children. She helped me find a job at the car factory she worked at in Minneapolis. The house I stayed at was full of men and their girls, and they were all Sierra Leoneans.

One of the men's friends, Sharif, took a liking to me. He would bring me drinks and weed when he came to visit. Sharif was kind of stocky with a bald head, not at all my type. He respected me, though, when I told him that I was not interested in a sexual relationship. Since I didn't have a car, he offered his help by driving me to the Department of Motor Vehicles to get a Minnesota Identification Card as well as to other faraway places. We eventually formed a strong, platonic friendship.

With three months of paystubs, I qualified to apply for low-income housing. Jennifer picked me up and drove me to St. Paul to put in my application for housing. While waiting to hear back about the apartment, Solo managed to find where I was staying and got a hold of the phone number.

One evening, I had just gotten home from work, and the phone rang. I picked it up, and it was Solo on the line. His first question was, "So you left Staten Island without telling me?"

"You told me it was over and I wanted a fresh start."

He must have thought we were still dating because he told me he wanted to join me in Minnesota. Silly me, I was thrilled because I felt like he wanted me now. He was choosing me over his daughter's mom. I wasn't even focusing on the physical, emotional, and mental abuse he had put me through. He went on and on about all the sweet things we could do together. I told him I was waiting on the apartment management to verify all my documents to get approved for my place.

By the time we got off the phone, plans were in motion for him to buy his Greyhound ticket to join me. A week later, Solo was on his way to Minnesota. I got approved for my first apartment in St. Paul's Skyline Tower on St. Anthony Drive at age twenty. The apartment was in my name, and it was on the fourteenth floor. The building had more than five hundred units and was the largest subsidized apartment complex in St. Paul.

Most of us who lived there were at the poverty level, and the building had a high crime rate. Many referred to it as "The Ghetto in the

Sky." Solo and I came from the Park Hill Projects, which was referred to as "Killer Hill" due to all the killings that happened there, so for us, Skyline Tower was a *better* place, an improvement.

Due to the excitement of being together again and having our own apartment, all we did was get high, drink, have sex, and work. I now worked as a certified home health aide, caring for elderly people at either retirement home facilities or the patients' homes. Solo became a drug dealer, selling to those within the building as well as the neighborhood. He also worked for staffing agencies. Unlike me, Solo never had a permanent job; it was always with staffing agencies. He didn't want a "nine-to-five" job. He worked when he *felt* like working. Plus, selling drugs was more profitable to him.

In the morning, I would go to my job while he stayed home to sell marijuana. Our apartment was always full of his friends when I got home from work. Whenever someone exited the elevator on our floor, all you smelled was weed smoke. Most of the time, it was coming from our apartment. You also could hear the loud noise of him and his friends playing cards or video games. I would join them while cooking for everyone. Solo became my everything.

Shortly after moving into our apartment, I started throwing up a lot, and I could not keep food in my stomach. Because of all the vomiting, I became seriously dehydrated and felt horrible. I had no idea what was wrong with me. I was fragile and could hardly stand on my own. I decided to go to the hospital, and Solo drove me in the Dodge Dynasty we had purchased with the money he made from selling weed. We arrived at St. Paul Ramsey Medical Center, and they immediately admitted me due to the dehydration. The nurse injected an IV and took some blood from me. I had no idea what was to come.

Chapter 8
Tutu

"No language can express the power and beauty and heroism of a mother's love"

- EDWIN CHAPIN

The doctor came into my room the next day to inform me that I was nine weeks pregnant. That was the scariest news I had ever heard. I was approaching my twenty-first birthday. I could not believe this was happening to me. My first thought was how my mom would react to this news. I had done nothing to prevent myself from getting pregnant. Solo and I had unprotected sex without thinking of the consequences. My life was such a blur with him. I was always high, constantly drunk. I burst out in tears after the doctor left my room.

How was I going to deliver the news to my family and Solo? I was kept in the hospital for twenty-four hours to gain strength. Solo did not stay by my side. He left right after they admitted me and told me to call him if I needed anything—as if being admitted to a hospital was not important enough. So he was not around when the doctor gave me the pregnancy results. I cried myself to sleep that night. Later the next day, Solo came to pick me up from the hospital. On the way home, he asked, "So, what did the doctor say was wrong with you?"

I took a deep breath and just above a whisper, I said, "I'm nine weeks pregnant."

Silence.

You could have heard a pin drop in that car. It was the longest drive of my life, and our apartment was about a twenty-minute drive from the hospital. But it felt like an eternity. When we pulled up to the apartment, Solo rolled a giant blunt. He took a drag and passed it to me, and I did the same.

After we finished smoking, he finally asked, "So, how much is it going to cost for an abortion?"

"What do you mean?" I asked.

"We are not keeping it."

"Oh, yes we are. I'm keeping it."

"I already have a daughter," he explained. "And I am not ready for another child."

"Well, you should have thought about that before having sex with me without protection." I stood my ground. "I'm not killing my baby!"

"Look, if you choose to keep the baby, I'm not going to be a part of it. I have one child and one child only."

That night, he slept in the living room while I slept in the bedroom. He wanted nothing to do with me because I was "disobedient." Our relationship went down the drain from there. The physical and emotional abuse went into a higher gear. I became a punching bag with every mistake I made or for talking back. I knew his intentions were for me to lose the baby, but the baby was here to stay.

I quit smoking cigarettes and drinking alcohol. However, I continued to get high on weed. The doctors would ask me if I had smoked weed. I would lie, but they knew. The evidence was in my blood work. To this day, I'm not proud of it. I was naive and scared. Smoking weed kept my nerves calm during those trying periods. I lived with a man who wanted nothing to do with our unborn child but would use my body as he saw fit when he wanted sex. I was miserable and in a toxic relationship. Not only was he abusive, but he also put my life in danger by selling drugs.

One day, two guys came to the apartment to buy marijuana, or so they said. But they knew that Solo kept all his drug money in the apartment. While I talked to one about the marijuana price, the other asked to use the bathroom, but he went to the bedroom instead and found where Solo kept his money. He grabbed the cash, came back out, and they rushed out of the apartment. I didn't know they had taken the money. I was so thankful they didn't do anything to me. When Solo came home and discovered the money was gone, he was furious.

"It wasn't my fault," I said. "I didn't know they knew you had money here."

He beat me up that day and left me with a black eye. When his friends came to our place, they saw me but none of them would say anything to him. Instead, they asked me what I did to upset him. With the pregnancy, me going against his wishes, and us living paycheck to paycheck, Solo was now constantly abusing me. But I was so insecure; I thought that was what I wanted—I thought it was love. The cops would show up at our apartment because we were disturbing the peace, yet I would tell them I was okay. I didn't want him to get into trouble. One night, the officers escorted him out of the building because they could see that I was not okay, but I also didn't want to press any charges on my unborn child's father. I didn't want him to have a police record.

The last straw came when I was about seven months into my pregnancy. That's when Solo held me at knifepoint. I think. Again, all of it was a blur because we were always so high. My friend Sharif, with whom Solo also was friends with, came to visit us like he always did. Unfortunately, on this visit, Solo was out. When he returned, he must have been high on something other than marijuana because he locked us all in a room, saying Sharif had impregnated me. He kept saying he wouldn't let us leave until we confessed that I cheated on him with Sharif. I was sitting there crying. Sharif was trying to convince him nothing sexual had ever happened between us, that he has cared for me as a younger sister. I was pleading for my life, the life of my unborn child, and for Sharif's life. I kept telling him I had never cheated on him. I had never looked at anyone else but him. He was the one I loved. Sharif kept begging and telling him that it was all a mistake. It was all in his head.

After some time, we finally convinced Solo of the truth, and he allowed Sharif to walk out of our room unharmed. That was the last time I saw Sharif in Minnesota. And I decided I would leave Solo after I gave birth. I called my mom and pleaded with her to forgive me. She had relocated to Milwaukee, Wisconsin and, like the entrepreneur she has always been; she had opened a 99¢ store. I explained my situation to her and the hell I had experienced living with Solo. She told me if I promised to return to college, she would take care of my baby. I promised. She forgave me and prayed for me to have a safe delivery.

Getting her blessing and assurance that I could go back home was all I needed to hear for me to leave Solo. Despite all the abuse I endured, Beatrice Weghar Carew ("Tutu" as we called her) was born on March 25, 1999. It was a hard labor and delivery. I arrived at the hospital in the morning on March 23, but she arrived naturally at 5:15 p.m. two days later, weighing five pounds and six ounces. She had marijuana in her system because I had smoked weed throughout my pregnancy. But, other than that, she was healthy. She had ten toes and ten fingers. My mom called the hospital after her birth and told me that as soon as I was strong enough, my sister Susan would come to pick me up and drive me down to Milwaukee with the baby.

A month later, Susan came, and we went to Milwaukee. When we arrived, my mom bolted out of the house running towards the car. I thought she was coming to hug me, but instead she reached inside the vehicle for Tutu. That was it. Tutu was hers from that moment. A month or so later, I went back to Milwaukee on a Greyhound bus, but this time with a different frame of mind. I enrolled at St. Paul Community College but dropped out a month after classes started because Solo had a problem with me going back to school. I knew there was no way I would change my life if I stayed with him. So, I told him that I was leaving him. Plus, the building management had given me an eviction notice—not because I didn't pay my rent, but because they found out Solo lived there and his name was not on the lease. In addition, all our fights, which disturbed the other tenants, made matters worse. So, I packed whatever I could take with me on the Greyhound bus and gave away the rest. I needed to empty the apartment so that I could turn in the key to the management office. Solo stayed in Minnesota with friends, and I left for Milwaukee. I finally realized he was not good for me and I needed to remove him from my life.

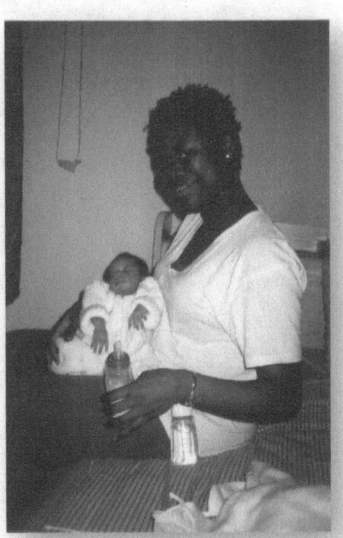

My oldest daughter Tutu at a couple of weeks old

Years later, I saw Solo again when he came to California on some drug deal. He had not changed his ways. He visited us and saw his daughter, who was about four years old at the time. He made all kinds of promises to Tutu but never kept them. He left, never for her to see him again. She still has yet to set eyes on him, as of this writing, and she is twenty-three years old now.

Interestingly, Solo saw my profile on social media and reached out to say, "I can't believe how you've changed. I don't recognize you."

"Well, I grew up."

Ignoring that comment, he said, "My daughter looks so beautiful."

I responded dryly, "Well, you didn't want her."

He has sent me friend requests. I've declined them. It's incredible how quickly things can turn around when you remove toxic people from your life.

Just My Tu Sense
(Lessons Learned)

———•••◆•••———

The minute your love interest, boyfriend, girlfriend, partner, or spouse starts calling you names, get out. If he or she even looks like they are raising a hand to hit you, get out. If you get hit and immediately receive apologies and/or gifts and reasons why, get out. Note: there are no good reasons to endure domestic abuse. Period! If your loved one promises they won't hit you again, leave. Honey, if you see ANY red flags, trust your instincts and get the hell out.

PART 4
MILWAUKEE, WISCONSIN

CHAPTER 9
MOVING BACK HOME

"I'm a lucky person because I've been loved a lot. I have a great family."
- MONICA BELLUCCI

After leaving home at nineteen and spending years in my own place, moving back in with my parents was humbling and hard. Tutu was about two years old and had been living with my parents since she was born. I was happy to be under the same roof with my baby girl. But I was twenty-two and I still smoked and drank. My parents had heard about my drinking and smoking but never saw me do either. After I moved back in with them, they had rules and number one was no smoking or drinking in their house. If I insisted on doing so, I would have to find an apartment. And because I didn't want to be restricted by any rules, I landed a job at an assisted living facility and senior care center ten minutes away from their home. I got certified as a nursing assistant and applied for food stamps and welfare. Getting certified was an eight-hour training course, but since I had prior experience in Minnesota, the center hired me right away. Even though my mom was entirely responsible for Tutu's well-being, she allowed me to keep my welfare benefits. Less than six months later, I rented a one-bedroom apartment. I was now working and receiving assistance, but I still lived paycheck to paycheck.

My bad habits of smoking and drinking were a huge part of my life. I started to ask my neighbors for cigarettes or marijuana. Most of my neighbors in my apartment complex were living the same lifestyle. We worked in the morning and smoked or drank for the rest of the day. Now and then, I would show up at my parents' house looking for something to eat or to say hello to my daughter. My mom knew I was up to no good, but she never said anything negative to me. She allowed me to be me.

One day, my baby sister Ella introduced me to her friend Kimberly, who unfortunately had the same bad habits. Ella was also a smoker, which I found out when I moved to Milwaukee. Kimberly was a mother of three or four kids but she liked to party. She became my party friend and one of the worst influences in my life.

Kimberly, Ella, and I would smoke weed together. During our smoking sessions, Ella would tell us stories of how *my* stepfather mistreated her after my mother left them in Liberia. The things she said made me paranoid about my daughter's safety with him. I didn't trust my stepdad, mainly because of my molestation in Africa. Ella never said anything about being molested by our stepdad, but she did say he would punish her severely when she did not do her chores. I started to see my stepdad as my mom's young brother, who used to abuse me physically. I thought he was maybe doing something to my daughter, abusing her in some way. As she grew older, I would ask Tutu if he touched her or had done anything inappropriate. All of this was coming from a place of fear. Even when my second daughter was born, I was not in a good place. I was always terrified for the well-being of my girls. It had taken years, until recently in my forties, when I finally apologized to my stepdad.

I know he truly loves my children the way a grandfather loves his grandkids. After years of living with them, I genuinely vow that my stepfather is one of the good ones. Yes, he screams and yells when he is upset, but none of us are angels. Tutu and Ophelia adore their grandfather. So I accept my stepdad for what he has shown me: a man who has stood by my mom's side through thick and thin for more than thirty years. It takes a special kind of man to marry a woman with four children and step into a fatherly role, even when we did not acknowledge him as our father for many, many years. I am blessed and thankful for his presence in our lives. While I have grown to accept and love my stepfather, there is one man who I will always regret being a part of my life and that's Percy.

Chapter 10
Percy

———•◆•———

"People inspire you, or they drain you. Pick them wisely."

- HANS F. HASEN

I met Percy when I walked into his clothing store in one of the most dangerous areas in Milwaukee. Stepping foot into that store changed the next ten years of my life. I didn't know it then, but it was the start of my journey from an insecure twenty-three-year-old to the strong and resilient woman I am today.

Percy was from Jamaica and one of Milwaukee's biggest marijuana drug dealers. He had a heavy accent, long dreadlocks, dark grayish eyes, and big teeth. He must have been in his late fifties or sixties, if not older. In his clothing store he sold skimpy and sexy outfits for women. It was a cover-up for what was happening in the back room. Pounds and pounds of weed were being bagged and prepared to be transported from Milwaukee to Jamaica Queens in New York.

There was nothing good about this man. He was a shot-caller and he was ruthless! If you were not part of his crew, you could be very intimidated being in his presence. He had a slender build but, with his gun always at his side, you wouldn't dare to cross him. He did not take lightly to someone fucking with his money or the people who made money for him. He only cared about himself. Now that I look back on it, he was very insecure and probably kept young girls like me around to feel good about himself.

Kimberly and I had gone to Percy's clothing store to buy some clothes to wear to the club. We wanted to be fly and turn heads when we stepped in the party. So at Percy's store we selected a few dresses and entered the fitting rooms to try them on. When I stepped out of the fitting room to get Kimberly's opinion, that's when Percy walked out from the back room, In his Jamaican accent he said, "Lawd have mercy. You are an African Goddess," or something to that effect. Kimberly and I were shocked because we were not expecting anyone else to be inside the store.

At this time, I too had long dreadlocks, was very slim and tall, and exotic in every way possible. He asked me what my name was and started to ask more questions. He loved the fact I was from Africa, the "motherland," as he put it.

"I would like to get to know you better."

He appeared to be a proper gentleman, but I knew he was not my type. Plus, he was old enough to be my father, and he was not good-looking. All of these were reasons for me not to entertain the idea of getting to know him. But by the time I left his store, we had exchanged phone numbers.

That Saturday, Kimberly and I arrived at the club around midnight, like we usually did, because the clubs didn't start jumping until later in the night. We bought our first drinks and started dancing on the dance floor. Guys began to join us, and we were having a grand time. Then I turned around and looked toward the bar, and there he was, Percy.

He looked like Mr. Biggs from the Isley Brothers, wearing a trench coat, a big hat with a feather on the side of it, and alligator shoes. I mean, if you know what a pimp dresses like, that was Percy. It should have been a red flag for me to keep my distance.

I whispered to Kimberly, "Look who's here."

"Oh girl, he came because of you."

"Yeah, right." I completely dismissed the idea because I was like, *what would this old man want from me? I have nothing to offer him*, so I thought nothing of it.

When the music stopped, I walked off the dance floor with the cute guy I was dancing with. Percy came over as we approached the bar and interrupted us by asking me to speak with him. Immediately I thought, *How rude. You see I'm talking to this young guy I am interested in, and here you come interrupting us.* But, of course, I was saying all this in my head.

He said, "Can I talk to you?"

"Um, sure." I was nervous and confused.

And for some reason, the young guy I was speaking with bolted like he had seen a ghost.

I joined Percy at the bar. He kept complimenting me, telling me how beautiful I was.

"You know, I can't stop thinking of me from the moment I saw you," he said. "You are a goddess, and you should be my girl."

I told him that he was too old for me, and I was not interested.

He said, "Do you want a young guy who can't offer you anything or an older guy who can take care of your needs?"

That got my attention, and he convinced me to visit him at his place of business.

After that night, I never thought I would see Percy again. I went about my life. Kimberly and I would work, then go out on Saturdays. It was what we did, especially when I knew my parents were caring for my daughter. Since my apartment was about ten minutes away, I visited my daughter when I could. I can honestly say that I was not a good mom during this time. Having fun and partying were priorities for me.

I checked in here and there, and my mother never really bothered me for anything regarding my daughter. I knew my baby girl was well cared for, so I never worried much about her.

I had forgotten about Percy, but he had not forgotten about me. A few weeks or so later, he showed up at the nightclub again and confronted me for lying to him. I had said I would visit him at his store and never kept my word. He told me he could offer me much more than what I was looking for at the nightclubs. As far as I was concerned, I was not interested in this man. But Percy set out to have me in his life.

As we were having this conversation, he took out a blunt, to my surprise, lit it, and started smoking right in front of me. Percy then passed me the blunt, asking if I would like to take a drag. I wondered how he knew I smoked weed. Without hesitation, I took it. That was a mistake because now he had me. I was young, naïve, and now vulnerable. That was one of the biggest mistakes I have made. Not just taking a hit of the weed but entertaining his conversation.

I promised Percy I would come to his business this time and talk some more. So as Kimberly and I danced, he kept a watchful eye on me. I didn't even want to dance with other guys because I could tell that Percy was the possessive type and wouldn't like to share anything with another. So I avoided any man that attempted to dance with me, playing it safe.

The moment came for us to say our goodbyes, and he decided to walk Kim and me outside. He then reminded me that he would be looking forward to seeing me soon, and he walked to his car, an old white limousine.

Kim was like, "Girl, he is driving a limousine."

It was not new, but it was a limousine, which was impressive to us youngsters at the time.

Kimberly and I talked about Percy during our drive home. *What is wrong with this man? He is crazy. What does he want with me? What is it about me?* Anyway, we laughed about the whole incident and never thought about it again.

A couple of days later, I kept my word and visited Percy at his store. He offered me a drink, but I declined. He passed me the blunt he was smoking. Of course, I started to smoke with him. Straight to the point, he asked me if I had ever considered being an exotic dancer. I told him that it was out of the question because of my family. He said that I dance so well it would be good to make money from it professionally. I continued to tell him it would bring shame to my parents, especially my mom's side, because of my upbringing and grandparents' names. He kept pushing the issue and said there was lots of money to be made. Plus, he would provide me with dancing costumes and everything I would need to get started. I continued to say I was not interested. He then shifted the conversation to my living arrangements and the cost of paying my rent and bills and caring for my daughter. I realized I was not making enough to survive. That's when what he was saying started to make more sense.

I was struggling to be a responsible person. Mind you, I could go to my parents' house if I was hungry or wanted a roof over my head. But it was my choice to be on my own. My mother was never a strict mom, and she was too busy running her business to care about what I was up to at that time. So when Percy showed me how he could help me make money and live a comfortable life, I believed him.

After I finally agreed to become a dancer, Percy came up with a master plan for me to move to his neighborhood. That was a big mistake because it gave him the upper hand to isolate me from my family, Kimberly, and everyone else I knew. But, of course, I wasn't thinking of that at the time.

I gave up my job and apartment and moved about two blocks from Percy's house, which he shared with his girlfriend/partner. We started visiting strip clubs outside of Milwaukee to watch other dancers and see their techniques. When it was finally time for me to go to clubs and audition, Percy would drive me. But when we got to the clubs, he would become distant because he didn't want the club owners or managers to know I was with him. I later found out that club owners or managers had zero tolerance for pimps or men who used young ladies to make money.

The strip club that hired me was a hole-in-the-wall club called the Cheetah Club in Milwaukee's Old North neighborhood. That part of town was dangerous. As a matter of fact, when you walked in, there was metal detector to go through. The Cheetah Club was the first and only strip club in Milwaukee I danced at. The dance name I chose was Rasta because I had dreadlocks, and I wanted to differentiate myself from the rest of the dancers. Being the only authentic African girl with dreadlocks was unique. And being unique made me stand out. The other dancers wore weaves and didn't look anything like me. Plus, Percy made sure the outfit I wore was like nothing anyone else had seen. It was the best from his store.

In hindsight, the Cheetah Club was for new dancers like myself, who had no idea what they were doing. It was not a fancy club like those you see in the movies. Instead, it was a place where young and older men found themselves when they were looking to release some stress or looking for someone to listen to their problems.

I was still insecure, and my self-esteem was low. The haunting words, 'You are so ugly' my aunt repeated on a regular basis were still in my head. It broke me inside for years. I thought I wasn't beautiful. So when I became a dancer and saw how men reacted toward me, drooling over me, made me feel good. My self-confidence went through the roof momentarily. I felt powerful. It gave me confirmation that I was indeed beautiful. Once dancing became my daily routine, Percy clarified that if a man was not paying for my time, I should not sit or talk with him. I was not to speak with any of the young guys because they had nothing to offer me.

As time went on, Percy only wanted me for himself. I was not allowed to talk to other guys inside or outside the club. Yes, he let me dance for other men, but he collected the money every night like a pimp. But to be clear, I never had sex with men for money. He was the only one who could touch me sexually, and he made sure of that. He would drop me off at the club to dance and pick me up afterward. I was his African girl toy, at his beck and call. It was crazy because he had women his age and even lived with a girlfriend. But he would leave her to come be with me, sometimes even spending the night.

Percy was methodical about how he operated. He isolated me from everyone in my life. I was not allowed to see my daughter, family, or Kimberly anymore. Since he provided for all of my basic needs, as far as he was concerned, I did not need anything else from outside sources. He now had complete control of every aspect of my life. He would sit there and watch my every move at the club, making me a nervous wreck. Percy would beat me if I talked to or gave another man more attention than they deserved. I was scared to death and walked on eggshells. He took advantage of my vulnerability. I didn't know what I had done to myself. It felt like I was living a nightmare and needed to wake up. I couldn't breathe. That's when I decided to get my freedom back.

I started speaking with guys at the club even though I knew they wouldn't pay me for my time. I talked more, made less money at the club, and became very disobedient toward Percy. When he drove me to the club, I would get out of the car without speaking. When he came into the club, I would keep my distance. By not acknowledging him, he became violent and even more possessive. He beat me with balled fists and had no problem calling me a bitch or bumbaclot! The beatings became constant. I felt like a dancing slave. I wanted to just leave, but I also knew that Percy didn't make idle threats. He would not think twice about finding me and ending my life. I was desperately looking for a way out. I needed a lifeline.

That's when Kenny caught my eye in the club.

Kenny was a light skinned black man in his late thirties and was very handsome. He stood about six feet three inches, with a great body. You would think that he was an NFL football player. Oh, and Kenny was a sweet talker. I saw him as my Prince Charming who was going to save me from the monster, Percy. I made it a habit to start a conversation with him when he came into the club, and he would buy me drinks. We talked during my breaks. Not once did he mention he was a pimp. Kenny was as ruthless as Percy, though I didn't know it at the time. From the frying pan into the fire, I jumped.

Percy noticed how Kenny flirted with me and I flirted back. I could see the raging emotions on Percy's face, but I didn't care. Kenny would always say that he wanted me as his girl. I always told him that I was already with someone, but he didn't know who that was.

The last straw in my "relationship" with Percy was when I got a ride from Kenny at the club. That night, Percy purposely did not come to pick me up on time. I waited for him and called him, but he didn't show up. Kenny offered me a ride to my apartment, and I accepted. I didn't know Percy was sitting across the street in his car watching. He followed us, and when we got to the apartment, I sat in the car talking to Kenny. Percy walked up to the passenger side, pointed his gun at me, and told me to get out of the vehicle. He then threatened Kenny that he would blow his brains out if he ever saw him even looking my way.

Percy then grabbed me by my hair and snatched me out of Kenny's car. I quickly pulled my dancing suitcase from the back seat and Kenny drove off. At 3:00 a.m., I was about to get the beating of my life. Percy forcefully pushed me into the apartment. He hit me on the head with the gun handle. The next thing I saw was blood dripping down my face from my head. I still have a scar on my scalp as a painful reminder of that pistol whipping. Then heavy blows and punches were coming at me right and left.

All the while, he screamed, "You ungrateful bitch! After everything me done for you, you disrespecting me? You allowed another man to see the place I spend my time with you? Do you have any idea what I am capable of doing to you? I would have fucking blown both of your brains out. You better thank your lucky stars I allowed him to leave with a warning."

He kept beating, kicking, and even biting me to the extent that I can still see his bite mark on my skin twenty years later. He also repeatedly raped me throughout the night. By the time daylight came, I could not recognize myself. That bastard casually walked out of the apartment and left me there for weeks. The only person who checked on me was his girlfriend.

She asked me, "Why did you push him to do what he did to you?" As if all of this was entirely my fault!

On her way out the door, she said, "Percy is vexed with you; I don't know when he will come over here again. You need to call him and apologize."

"*No, I need to get the fuck out of here,*" I thought to myself.

Since she didn't know when he would come back, I saw it as a chance at freedom. It was my opportunity to escape, and I took it.

Chapter 11
Into The Fire

"Turn your wounds into wisdom."

- OPRAH WINFREY

I called Kenny and explained everything that happened with Percy.

"Ok, I'm on my way to pick you up," he said. "Pack your stuff and be ready when I get there."

"But everything is Percy's. I just have a few things," I said while frantically grabbing the only items I did own: my clothes, shoes, family pictures, and documents. "Please hurry. If Percy finds me, he's gonna kill me, and I definitely can't ever show my face inside the Cheetah Club again."

"Don't worry. I got you." Kenny assured. "You'll be safe with me."

In about an hour, Kenny showed up and drove me to his house in a different part of Milwaukee.

In less than a couple of weeks, he rented me an apartment. I was so naive thinking Kenny was doing this for me out of the goodness of his heart. The notion of Prince Charming rescuing me from a demonic man disappeared once I realized Kenny's true intentions. He did not want me to be his girlfriend. He wanted me to sell my body for him. Kenny wanted me to dance and sleep with men. He took the pimping game as I knew it to a whole other level. At least Percy wanted my body only for himself. Kenny was a real pimp and wanted me to sell my body, actually have sex for money. His exact words were: "You have to pay my dues." According to him, he did not put his life on the line to save me from Percy not to keep me for himself.

I hated myself. Here I go again! How did I seem to attract these types of men? How could I get out of this new mess? My life was becoming hopeless by the minute. I hated everything about myself.

Why didn't I recognize the red flags? I can't be this stupid, I would say to myself. But, here I was, a naive twenty-four-year-old in a horrible situation. Kenny, like Percy, also had a girlfriend, and she was a professional dancer. She also had children, and they were partners in finding girls and making them work for them. Kenny's girlfriend never danced in the Wisconsin area. She danced in other states. Kenny made her take me along on one of her trips since Percy was still searching for me. I knew he was looking for me because I'd get threatening phone calls, which always had me looking over my shoulder.

On my first trip to North Dakota, Kenny's girlfriend introduced me to clubs and showed me how to make money from men. The club owners paid out-of-state dancers weekly because they traveled far to work at their clubs. There was no need for extra activities like selling your body. The club payments and tips were enough, plus I flat out refused to sleep with men for money. When that bit of news got back to Kenny, he was not happy. He told his girlfriend to leave me and go to South Dakota to dance.

I felt free because I didn't have her watching my every move and reporting to him. But, I was scared because I was by myself in a strange state where I didn't see many people who looked like me, except for the dancers. Most black dancers chose North Dakota because they knew men paid a lot of money to spend time with black women. I found that to be true when an angel walked into the club named Michael.

Michael was a short white man, probably about five foot six, with a bald head and stocky build. He came in dressed up in a suit and tie, not like the typical regulars at the club. I had just gone up onstage. He opened the door; the light from outside came in with him because it was about 4:00 p.m. He walked straight up to the stage, stood close by, and stared at me for a while.

He then tipped me and asked, "Would you mind joining me for a few minutes when you get off stage? I just want to talk to you."

"Sure, okay," I said.

"So, what would you like to drink?" he yelled so I could hear him over the music.

I got a little closer to him so he could hear me say, "Guinness Stout."

He went to the bar and ordered my drink and got himself water with lime. After I got offstage, I walked around the club thanking everyone who had tipped me onstage, and then I joined Michael.

His first words were, "Wow, you are beautiful. What's your name?"

"Rasta," I said.

"I don't meet many dancers with the name Rasta."

"I know. I'm unique." I smiled.

"I can see that," he said.

That's how our friendship began. Michael was kind, loving, and never treated me like a dancer. Every time he visited me at the club, we talked about my family and why I chose to be a dancer. On my days off from work, Sundays, Michael would pick me up and take me to restaurants, take me shopping, or just drive around to show me Bismarck. He seemed very proud to walk around town with me. When I was with him and people stared, he would tell me to ignore them; that they must not have seen a beautiful black woman before.

Michael was a well-to-do businessman, but he never seemed to care about what others thought of our friendship. I was always at my happiest when with him. I never had to dance or do anything for him to give me money. He wanted to spoil me, and I let him. With him, I sometimes forgot I was in North Dakota for work.

Soon my dancing contract was over, and it was time for me to return to Milwaukee and face Kenny. Michael gave me his contact information if I needed anything or if I ever returned to North Dakota. We said our farewells because I didn't know if I would see him again.

The following day, I took a cab to the Amtrak train station to head back to Milwaukee. During the day-and-a-half trip, I contemplated what I would tell Kenny and how he might react to me not doing what he wanted. I could never bring myself to sell my body. Nope. That was a line I simply would not cross, so I would just have to suffer the consequences. I figured it couldn't be worse than what I had already endured with Percy.

I arrived at the train station in downtown Milwaukee late at night, and Kenny was there waiting for me. He had the key to my apartment, which meant there was no way I could avoid him, plus the apartment was in his name. I made it to the passenger's arrival area, and he grabbed my suitcase, which was mainly my dancing clothes and things Michael had bought me. We got into the car, and the first thing that met my face was a punch. I never saw it coming. I blacked out, and when I regained consciousness, he had driven me to a part of Milwaukee I didn't recognize. He reached into his glove compartment, took out his gun and pointed it at my left temple.

"I can kill you right here, dump your body and go about my business," he said with an evil grin. "Bitch, the next time you disrespect me, this is where your body will end up."

I was only twenty-four years old and already two men had threatened my life with guns, and another with a knife.

We headed back to my apartment—well, his apartment. In the car he slapped and punched me and called me "bitch this" and "bitch that" endlessly. He then dragged me out of his car into the apartment, and that's when the torture intensified. He tied me up with a rope and left me in the apartment to think about what I had done by refusing to sell myself for him. He kept saying he should have left me with Percy. I told myself, *yes, you should have left me with Percy because at least he wanted me for himself.*

He said, "Do you think you're better than all the girls working for me and paying their dues?"

I had no response. I knew I had to repay him one way or the other for saving me from Percy. If I didn't, I would find myself on the other side of the tracks. He then took all the money I brought with me from North Dakota and left me tied up in the closet. I had lost track of the day and time. The next time I saw him was when he brought me food to eat. He went through my suitcase and took all the things Michael had bought me, which made him even more upset, because that's money Michael could have given me instead. For that reason, I received more slaps.

He went into my closet and took all my best clothes, shoes, and family pictures (because I had expressed to him how much it meant to me to surround myself with my family pictures) and put them in his car. He then took my so-called worthless items, tossed them into the bathtub, and poured Clorox bleach and fingernail polish all over them. He left me with a pair of jeans, two sweaters, a jacket, a pair of sneakers, and my dance suitcase full of my dancing outfits. He said he would keep what he took at his place until I started acting right. He untied me and said I would return to dancing as soon as I healed or my bruises disappeared.

"I hope you've learned your lesson and don't ever fuck with me or my money."

At the time my family lived in Milwaukee. But since Percy isolated me from them, I didn't want to reach out. Come to find out, my mother had searched for me and tried to get a hold of me. I didn't want to be around her or my daughter. I felt like such a disgrace. I didn't want to see the disappointed faces of my entire family because being an exotic dancer is unheard of in my African culture.

My mom called my cell phone and left an urgent message that they were relocating to California to open an African convenience store, and she was taking my daughter. I had no option but to return her call. The next thing I knew she had invited herself over to my apartment. When my mom arrived with my daughter, Tutu, who was almost three years old at the time, she was in disbelief that I had allowed myself to get to this level. She asked me if I cared at all about my daughter growing up without her mother around. Yes, I did care, and I wanted my daughter to grow up with me around.

My mom spoke with a mixture of anger and sadness. The next thing she said haunts me to this day: "I don't want the police to call me one day to come and identify your body."

The condition that my mom saw me in, black and blue from Kenny's beatings, she knew if I didn't get away from him, the next time she would see me would be in a body bag. Every time I remember that I get chills up and down my body. My mom had saved my life by saying those chilling words to me. That's what I needed to hear. I agreed to leave Wisconsin with them and move to California.

Chapter 12
Mom

"A mother is the truest friend we have when trials, heavy and sudden, fall upon us; when adversity takes the place of prosperity."

- WASHINGTON IRVING

From the day I made the decision to leave Wisconsin, my mom became my rock and we truly started to bond as mother and daughter. I mean, I have always admired my mom and her unrelenting drive. She had to be in her early twenties when she left her kids to pursue her dreams. A natural entrepreneur, she didn't have a degree, but she was street smart and business savvy. My mom essentially started an export/import business by herself. She'd travel and buy items and turn around and sell them for a profit. Once we came to the United States, she went from being a home health aide to the owner of a 99 Cent Plus store. Talk about a business hustler. She was the ultimate hustler and I'm sure I get my entrepreneurial drive from her. Of her four daughters, despite my lifestyle, I was the one who was always there. I'm sure it was mostly because she was raising my daughter, but if she needed me, I was there while my sisters were living their lives elsewhere.

With all that I had been through, my mom was always there with open arms and never judged me. Okay, there was one time she had quite a few choice words for me when she learned I was pregnant with Tutu out of wedlock. But regarding my dancing, my mother only wanted me to be safe; she cared less about me being an exotic dancer. And to think, the whole time I stayed away I was worried she would be upset with what I did for a living. It was all in my head. My mother only wanted her daughter back, but I had allowed men to destroy me. All the same, I was willing to give it another try and start all over again. I grabbed my dance suitcase, got dressed, and walked away from the apartment that Kenny rented for me. And I never looked back.

I stayed in Milwaukee for another week because my parents had to make arrangements for the rental trucks. I received a lot of threatening phone calls from Kenny, which led me to stay close to home and spend some quality time with my daughter for the first time in a very long time.

I had become a woman I didn't recognize when I was an exotic dancer, allowing Kenny and Percy to abuse me physically, emotionally, and mentally. As I look back now, I know all the marijuana smoking clouded my judgment. Both men made it available to me any time I wanted it. Plus, I drank liquor like it was water. Over the years, I found comfort in the bottle. These two bad habits helped me zone out onstage to withstand what was happening.

My mom asking me to move to California with them was my saving grace and a huge turning point in my life. I left Milwaukee, Wisconsin, with nothing but a few clothes and my driver's license. Still, the last week of December 2000, I was in a Budget truck leading my parents to California. The Golden State would be a new beginning for me.

My mom's first visit back from America to Sierra Leone and ended up bringing my old sister back to America with her

Just My Tu Sense
(Lessons Learned)

Be leery of any man who wants to take care of all your basic needs in exchange for anything. In my case it was dancing.

Know that any drugs you take, whether legal or illegal for an extended period of time, will affect you and your decision making.

Your body should not be anybody's punching bag.

PART 5
HAWTHORNE, CALIFORNIA

Chapter 13
A Clean Slate

"A dream doesn't become reality through magic; it takes sweat, determination and hard work."

- COLIN POWELL

We arrived in California on January 1, 2001, at night. My daughter, mom, stepdad, cousin, and I left Milwaukee in a blizzard. All the adults were driving Budget trucks loaded with convenience store goods. It was a very long trip, and I was, of course, leading the pack with just a printed map. Nevertheless, the trip was an incredible experience because my parents believed in me to lead them to California. And we did arrive safely.

On the way, I had plenty of time to reflect on how my mom saved me from yet another abusive relationship. She saw I was a battered woman. God has been protecting me all along. The day my mom came to my apartment was all God's doing. I didn't even think twice when she asked me to relocate with them to California. I made a promise to myself I would never put myself in that type of situation again. Coming to California would be a clean slate for me and I was going to approach it with a different mindset.

The move, however, was not as easy as we thought it would be. We were to stay with my mom's older brother, his wife, and her adult son. My uncle and his wife had a three-bedroom house in Inglewood, but it was not large enough for all of us. My auntie, whom I had never met before, is African American. Other than seeing her pictures and speaking with her over the phone, we didn't know her too well. Her demeanor changed as days and weeks passed by with all of us under the same roof. I could tell we were cramping her style. She argued with my uncle about us overstaying our welcome.

I told my mom, "I can't do this anymore; I'm going back to North Dakota for a dancing gig because I need money."

"Just hold on until we find a storefront, and then you can go," my mom said.

My parents and I searched for a storefront location for a month, but it was tough because we were still out-of-towners. In addition, the process of changing all our legal documents was challenging. I remembered going to the Department of Motor Vehicles to get my California driver's license, but they needed other documents. That's when it hit me: Kenny had kept my green card, Social Security card, and everything else that was valuable to me. Moreover, he had me looking over my shoulder everywhere I went. Almost daily my phone would ring, I'd answer and it was him saying, "Bitch, watch your back," or "When I find you, you're a dead bitch," or "You think you can hide from me?"

I was always worried that he would find me one day, which would be the end of me. But I didn't allow the fear to stop me. My number one goal was to get my documents back. To move forward in my life I needed those identification cards. I would eventually need a California driver's license if I wanted to get a place of my own.

God worked things out, though. My parents found a store space on Crenshaw and 135th Street in Hawthorne. It was about three thousand square feet with a loft area on the second level for storing goods. We moved into the store at the end of February. Downstairs was my parents' business, called International African Market, and upstairs was our sleeping space. We decided it was better to sleep inside the store instead of making my aunt and uncle uncomfortable and having endless fights. So at night, when we closed the store, all four of us went upstairs and slept. We would get dressed quickly in the morning before the shops in our plaza opened for business. We lived in my parent's store for at least six months, or at least my parents did, because I left for North Dakota.

I had thought, *Okay, although it's not ideal, we now have a space to sleep, but I need to get my documents back*. I decided to work in North Dakota for two weeks and make some quick money. The club would pay dancers $1400 for two weeks. We had to pay the DJ and the bouncers, but the rest of the money was mine. Plus, dancers kept all of their tips and I made great tips. On a good night, I was taking home a couple grand in tips alone.

This time around, I was dancing on my terms. There would be no man or wannabe pimp to take my money. I would then be able to apply for a duplicate green card and get a Social Security card. I was determined to take control of my life and get back all Kenny took away from me.

I booked a two-week gig and then called Michael to tell him I would be in North Dakota for work. He was excited I was returning. On the day of my departure, my mom and Tutu dropped me off at the Greyhound bus depot. I boarded the bus for the long journey to Bismarck, North Dakota.

Three days or so later, I arrived, called for a cab to my motel room, checked in, and took a very long shower. I had not taken a shower since my family had moved into the store. You have no idea how amazing it felt to shower after going without it for many months. Washing up with soap and water from the sink does not compare. It was a fantastic feeling to have water pouring down my body from the showerhead. Afterward, I slept for the rest of the day.

The following day, I called Michael and told him I had arrived safely. He said he would come over during his lunch break and take me out for lunch. When he picked me up, we went to Red Lobster. I shared with him everything I endured at the hands of Kenny and how he had kept all my documents I needed to prove I was legally in this country.

"I left Milwaukee with just the few clothes I had on and my suitcase full of dancing clothes and shoes," I explained. "The only reason I'm back in Bismarck is to make money to get duplicates of my documents." I didn't know how I was going to go about it, but I needed money.

To my surprise, Michael knew people in high places. He drove me to an office building in downtown Bismarck the next day. I can't remember what type of office building it was. Still, I knew it was a high-profile office because I left with an official letter for me to take to the immigration office in California. To this day, I don't know who that person was who gave me the official letter, but I know Michael knew him, and he was a big deal in North Dakota.

I remember leaving that building feeling relieved and hopeful. I had peace of mind knowing that when I returned to California, there was a possibility I would get my documents back. For the rest of the week, I worked at the club in order to fulfill my contract and then hung out with Michael. He took me fishing and camping along the Mississippi River, which, by the way, was my first time doing both things and was an amazing experience. No one had ever exposed me to outdoor activities, and I must admit, it was refreshing to be able to do something like that.

Michael got to know me on a personal level outside the club. He began to know me as Mariatu, not the dancer, Rasta. His intentions were genuine for me as Mariatu, the young woman trying to find herself and get her stuff together. He advised me to go back to school and get out of the dancing game.

On my last night dancing in North Dakota, Michael came to give me a book and said farewell. The book was *The Seven Spiritual Laws of*

Success by Deepak Chopra. He signed it, "To Mariatu, you deserve the best of everything. Michael." I still have that book today, all these years later. I've read it so many times. It has played a huge role in my transformation. It changed my life.

Michael sat with me for a while at the club and told me of all the good qualities he saw in me, and I promised him I would give up dancing and go back to school. Then Michael decided to take off. I hugged him, and then went onstage to perform. Although it was not the last time I spoke with Michael, that was the last time I would see him. At the end of the night, the club paid me for my two-week contract. The next day, I took a cab to the Greyhound bus depot for my three-day journey back to California. As I sat in that bus seat looking out the window, I knew I was never returning to North Dakota. I took all the good memories I shared with Michael. Today, he is in his early seventies. I see him on Facebook. I am glad he can see how I transformed my life and that his help was not in vain.

My goal was to make something of myself as I had promised him I would. Although it was not going to be easy, I planned on doing just what I had pledged. I arrived in downtown Los Angeles, and my mom and Tutu were there to pick me up. Tutu, in her car seat, was excited to see me, and so was my mom.

After being gone for two weeks, I dreaded the idea of sleeping in the store with my parents again. So, I got a room at one of the sleaziest motels on Prairie Avenue in Inglewood. I could afford a better hotel, but I wanted to save most of my money. I just needed a place to sleep that had a bathroom where I could take a nice, hot shower. In fact, my mom and my daughter would come over to the motel to take showers while my dad used the store restroom.

One day on my way to the store, I noticed a few ladies dragging suitcases inside this building that looked like your basic, nondescript bar. There's only one reason I could think of for women with suitcases going into a "bar."

Chapter 14
King Henry VIII

"The shy and the extroverted have this in common—that they both fancy they are the center of attention."

- ROBERT BRAULT

As I stepped inside King Henry VIII, I blinked to adjust my eyes as it was dark, with just the stage lights illuminated. It was also pretty much empty except for the staff, one waitress, the cook, and the DJ. The bartender was preparing for the club to open. I was nervous because I had no idea what to expect. After all, this was the first strip club in California I had ever visited. Compared to some of the hole-in-the-wall clubs I had performed at, King Henry was much larger and sophisticated. When you walked in, there was an actual DJ area, the bar, of course, and a real stage with a stripper pole. I was impressed.

I made my way to the bar with my dance bag in hand and asked the bartender, whose name I overheard was Sweeney, if they were hiring dancers.

"We're always hiring dancers. You have time to audition?"

"Yes," I said.

He pointed to the dressing room and told me to change. The dressing room was huge and I immediately noticed the lockers that were available for dancers. The other dancers had not arrived yet so I had it all to myself. In less than twenty minutes, I switched from my street clothes into my dancing costume. By this time, I was pretty much a veteran in the game, so I came with one of my best outfits, a bikini with a dress made out of chains to go over it. The finishing touch on this money maker getup was my 8-inch clear stiletto heels. I did my makeup, complete with glitter eye shadow and bold, bright lipstick. I went out to the back patio to smoke because I needed to calm my nerves.

When I stepped back into the club, more dancers had arrived. The club was now open, and a few gentlemen were already sitting at the bar. Sweeney told me to tell the DJ my dance name and the music I would like. After a short conversation with the DJ, I sat at the bar, and Sweeney gave me a shot of his special drink. It was sweet and you hardly tasted the alcohol, but it packed a punch. Shortly after, I heard my name over the speaker.

"Coming up next on stage is Rasta!"

My heart jumped!

I walked to the backroom to go onstage. When I heard my music come on, I pranced across that stage and danced my heart off because I wanted the job so badly. Making ends meet was a priority. I got offstage after dancing to two songs. Although there were only three or four men in the club, they all threw dollars my way while I worked the stage. That was the confidence boost I needed.

I walked up to Sweeney, and he said, "Can you start now?"

I smiled and said, "I sure can."

That was the beginning of my dancing in California. For the first time, I was dancing for myself, and not just a two-week gig. All the money I earned was going to be mine and mine alone. So I would put in my full, one-hundred-percent effort.

King Henry wasn't the only strip club I danced at in Los Angeles County. I performed in different clubs, from hole-in-the-walls to high-end clubs. But King Henry was the one I was mainly known for. It was my home base. Plus, it was conveniently located. My apartment, which I was finally able to afford, was nearby and my mom's store was just a block away. It was so close that Sweeney would stop by the store on the way to the club.

He would say, "Rasta, what's up?"

I had introduced him to my mom and the rest of my family. He would chit-chat and buy cigarettes or something. It was an interesting dynamic. In the store he was able to see me as Tu, a mother and a daughter. At the club, he saw me as a bad ass stripper named Rasta.

When we were in the club, it was all business. Our conversations were work-related only. Plus, I was very selective about who I talked to in the strip club.

I paid attention to the type of men that came in, especially at King Henry or high-end clubs. Because of my experience with Percy and Kenny, I stayed away from the Caribbean and African American men. It was white men who seemed to be drawn to me anyway. And I loved their admiration. They treated me like I was a beautiful African queen, which did wonders for my self-esteem after having it engrained in my mind that I was ugly. While black men like Percy and Kenny dogged me and treated me like property, white men like Michael adored me and showed me nothing but the utmost respect. Even when I danced, I gravitated toward white men and they were mesmerized by me.

Dancing came naturally for me due to my upbringing. In African culture, everything we do includes music and singing, even burials. We wore colorful skirts and dresses and moved to beats coming from handmade drums, tambourines, and other instruments that sounded like maracas. Dancing was also a significant part of everything in the good and bad times. Since my grandparents were well to do, there were always parties and traditional performances at the house with music, singing, and dancing. So I guess that stayed with me. However, at this point in my life, dancing was about survival. I knew, though, I wasn't going to do it for the rest of my life. I had met women twice my age who were still dancing. For them, shaking their asses was their daily hustle. For me, I was just passing through to get to my ultimate destination.

During my dancing years, I met men at the clubs whom I dated for short periods. But, there was no way I could build a strong relationship with a man that met me in a strip club. It was always about the money, nothing more. There were no emotional feelings attached to the men I met at the club. And certainly not love. It was all about hustling. Some thought they were Prince Charming and wanted to save me. Some were good men who didn't want to take advantage of me and truly had good intentions. Men like Charlie.

Charlie was an elderly gentleman who seemed to like the young girls around him. When he saw me dance for the first time, he asked Sweeney about me.

"That's Rasta," he said. "She's African."

That must have intrigued Charlie. He threw a bunch of money at me onstage—something men did when they wanted to get a dancer's attention.

I went to him after I got offstage and thanked him for the tip. He offered to buy me a drink, and we started talking. My meeting Charlie was life changing. We started seeing each other regularly outside the club. He owned an auto parts company, and we would meet in his office. Charlie was in his seventies, and I was in my late twenties. I told him about my life and how I was a single mom. He became my sugar daddy and met all my needs except sexually, of course. But at the time, I didn't care. I was not in it for sex. Charlie wanted companionship outside the club, and

I was there to provide it. In turn, he took care of me and my daughter, whom he made sure I enrolled in a private kindergarten school. He also had me enroll in cosmetology school and paid for all expenses. He gave me an American Express card to buy whatever I needed for my beauty school supplies. When I moved into a one-bedroom apartment in Hawthorne, Charlie generously paid for all my household expenses.

I chose to go Beauty College because my sister Ella and I had braided hair for a shop in Milwaukee for extra cash. The shop owner would pay us a commission for every client we had. It wasn't something I was interested in doing long-term because it was time-consuming, but it kept money in my pocket, especially to support my smoking and drinking habits. I only did that for a year until I met Percy, who eventually isolated me from that too. Back in Africa, I had braided my girlfriends' hair; it was how I discovered my passion for hair. So pursuing a career in cosmetology made sense.

I attended John Perry Beauty College for nine months: September 2004 through June 2005. I would go to class in the morning and dance at King Henry the VIII at night. That was the only strip club I danced at during my time in Beauty College. When I graduated, I took the cosmetology exam. I passed the practical but failed the written portion. I retook the written exam six months later, and I received my cosmetology license on November 4, 2005. After that, I started doing hair in Gardena and eventually got a booth.

During my waiting period to retake my exam, Charlie pushed me to enroll in college. So I started taking business classes at El Camino Community College in Torrance. My mind was not on school, though. I was still drinking and smoking heavily at this time. Dancing also consumed my life. For me to get through the night—to feel comfortable on stage—I had to drink and smoke a lot. I'm not proud of it, but there were days where I would leave the club so intoxicated that I don't remember getting home.

Completing beauty school was a huge accomplishment, but I was still fighting my demons and drowning in alcohol. Hennessey and Guinness Stout were my poisons of choice. Even with all my power over men as a stripper, I was still insecure and felt like I was ugly, yet another reason to drink. Michael could not save me from me. And Charlie could not save me from me. I had to do that all on my own.

Chapter 15
A New Beginning... As a Business Owner

"Being the narrator of your life allows you to create new beginnings any time you want."

- UNKNOWN

One day, I was having breakfast at an IHOP in Gardena with Tutu when I noticed a "For Sale" sign at a small salon across the street. The lady was selling it for $5,000. *Who sells something like that for just $5,000?* I would find out later—after taking over the salon—exactly why. The salon had three stations and a shampoo bowl. It also had products in the display cabinet that I found out later were all expired, unfortunately.

I was so excited about owning my own business. I went to Charlie and told him I had found a salon for sale. In true Charlie fashion of spoiling me, he didn't even question if it was a good idea. We met up with the salon owner, and in about a week, I was officially the new owner of a beauty salon. I drove down to the Los Angeles County Registrar-Recorder office on La Cienega Boulevard to register my fictitious business name: Tu Studio Hair Designs. Charlie paid for all the renovations on the property and bought all new furniture and supplies needed for my start-up. In November 2006, Tu Studio Hair Designs was open for business.

Now I was doing three things: dancing at night, doing hair during the day, and in between, I was taking classes at El Camino College, which, fortunately, was walking distance from work.

Looking back, I should have known what was to come with the salon as I didn't have any idea about running a business. I was blinded by the excitement of owning my own business. I saw it as a way to get out of the dancing game and an opportunity to be able to support myself. I was swept up by the glamour of it all, but ultimately it was a bad idea. First, the salon was in the wrong location. It was in a predominantly Vietnamese area. Second, I didn't have any business sense, and I was just a year out of beauty school. As a result, the only regular customer I had was the person who bought me the business, which did help me practice my men's haircut skills.

Meanwhile, my family finally moved out of the store. For the first time since moving to California, we were able to celebrate Thanksgiving and Christmas in an apartment. Things were falling into place. I was in school. My parents' business was booming. I was becoming more popular at King Henry VIII. And the other dancers now knew I did hair at my salon and were becoming clients. My family and I had excellent places to lay our heads at night. Everything was good.

Through all the struggles, my mom never once looked down on me. Even if pole dancing was against our culture, she saw it as sustaining myself. All she would tell me was not to get mixed up with a wannabe pimp again. "Make money for yourself," she said.

I was doing just that until Charlie fell ill. I realized something was wrong when he didn't send me flowers for my birthday like he always did. I eventually found out he had been in the hospital. I was shocked and made my way to visit him. At that time, his wife (yes, he was married) only knew me as his barber.

Once Charlie died, everything died. His wife found out about our relationship and was furious. The American Express card he gave me as a second cardholder had left behind a paper trail. That's how she found out. She was a woman scorned and rightly so. She took me to court to pay for all the things Charlie had paid for me. The judge ruled in the wife's favor. So I had to pay her back. There was no way I could pay it as a lump sum, so I made payment arrangements with her. I was hustling to pay my bills and to pay her.

Then the Great Recession hit in 2008. It affected so many things—homeowners and the gentlemen's clubs. Men stopped coming in as much. Sometimes there were only the dancers in the club, just sitting around waiting. I had one booth renter at the salon, but she always had excuses why she could not pay me. Things were starting to fall apart. Charlie was no longer with me, the club was no longer busy due to the market crash, and the booth renter at my salon took advantage of my not-so-knowledgeable way of running a business.

If I knew then what I know now, I would have been a millionaire. I made a lot of money as a stripper, and not once did I save or invest the money I made. As a dancer, you could make $1,000 or more per night and most dancers, including me, would spend it all because they knew they would make it all back the next night. So I was making money left and right, and spending it left and right.

I wanted to keep the salon so bad, but I couldn't afford the payment, the apartment rent, and the car payment. So I finally gave up my apartment and moved into my salon, just like my family had done at my mom's store when we first moved to California. It was a full circle moment.

Now that Charlie had passed, I was fully invested in dancing because I needed to pay my bills. I would dance and then sneak into my salon to sleep there every night. I was essentially homeless and no one knew. My mom would ask me, "Why are you acting like you don't have a home?"

When she found out I was living in the salon, she asked, "Why would you give up your apartment?"

"Well, I couldn't afford to pay for both the salon and the apartment. One of them had to go."

She told me they had a four-bedroom house in Fontana. I didn't have to sleep in the salon. I could live with them.

I wanted to hold on to what Charlie had put so much money into. I didn't want to lose my salon.

My mother said, "If God wants you to own another salon someday, you'll get another one."

After a few weeks, I gave in and finally took her advice. I called my landlord and told him I couldn't afford the rent. I was in over my head, and the economy had taken a toll on me. I told him to keep the deposit. He was a good landlord. He was nice enough to allow me to remove all my furniture and fixtures from the salon, all of which Charlie had brought. I moved them all into my mom's garage. I was hoping to open another salon in the future. Upon leaving Hawthorne and moving to Fontana, I made a promise to never again allow myself to depend on someone so much and to never get involved with a married man. Ever!

Just My Tu Sense
(Lesson Learned)

Even when you have people to rescue you, ultimately your mindset must be that of rescuing yourself.

They say, "tough times don't last but tough people do." I believe that. You are tougher than you think. Keep going in the pursuit of your dreams.

PART 6
INLAND EMPIRE

Chapter 16
Leaving Dancing Behind

"There's a trick to the graceful exit. It begins with the vision to recognize when a job, a life stage, a relationship is over and let go. It means leaving what's over without denying its values."

- ELLEN GOODMAN

Even though I had moved to Fontana, I went to Hawthorne every Friday and Saturday to dance at King Henry VIII. I hopped on the Metrolink train to Union Station and then took the Los Angeles Metro to Crenshaw Boulevard. From Crenshaw, it was a five-minute taxi drive to King Henry VIII. I would stay with a friend on those nights and return to the IE on Sunday. Unfortunately, with the recession still going on, there wasn't much money left after paying the club fee, DJ, and bouncer.

It was a huge a waste of my time to make the trek down to Los Angeles for work. Every trip became increasingly discouraging. By this time, I had been a licensed cosmetologist for four years. I just wasn't working in my field. But with the slowdown at the strip club, I figured it was time to make use of my license again. After scouring job postings, I applied for a hairstyling position at Fantastic Sams, even though I wasn't experienced with doing the type of hair Fantastic Sams customers had.

Nor was I an expert at haircuts and color, which are top services at the popular franchise. When I received the call for an interview, I was both excited and nervous. By the grace of God I got hired and the manager assigned me to their busiest location in Upland, which sealed the deal for me not to return to King Henry VIII. After ten years, I had finally given up dancing for good!

Fantastic Sams offered free training to all their employees at that time. It was up to the employees to sign up and attend the classes. Let me tell you, I signed up for every training, including how to become a top seller for their retail products. Life at this company was starting to take shape. I was beginning to feel proud of myself and my career. But I couldn't shake the feeling that I needed to go back to school and actually finish.

One day as I conversed with a client, she mentioned Chaffey College and had lots of positive things to say. That's all I needed to hear. In September of 2009 on my day off I took two buses and went to the Chaffey admissions office in Rancho Cucamonga to submit my college application.

After applying I met with the financial aid staff. Because I was still on public assistance, they said I was eligible for the CalWorks program. I dedicated the whole day to making sure all my applications were submitted.

By Chaffey's winter session, January 2010, I was officially back in college again. I had dropped in and out of college throughout my twenties. This time, I was determined to graduate with an associate's degree. However, my life changed while at Chaffey, and it started with my first encounter with Professor Thierry Brusselle's "Intro to Business" class. At first, I was quiet in his class. Then, one day, I did poorly on his class exam, which led me to go to his office and speak with him about my grade. Thierry had an open-door policy for all of his students.

Once I knew I could visit him during his office hours to discuss my class grades, class projects, and school issues, I took advantage of the opportunity. He encouraged all of his students, including me, to visit our professors' offices. He made me understand that reaching out to your professors for guidance is essential for becoming a better student. He admired how I carried myself and came to class early, even though I took two buses, sometimes three, depending on if I had to go from school to work. Still, I never missed his early morning class. And, trust me, it was not easy waking up early in the morning to walk to a bus stop, rain or shine, to make it to that 8:00 a.m. class, but I did it. If I didn't do well, I would retake his exams to get better grades.

"I don't know why other students are not like you," he said.

I started to understand that he cared for his students and wanted to see them excel no matter what. Thierry had no idea I was a struggling single mother on welfare. Instead, he saw a student who gave a hundred percent in everything school-related. He became even more determined to guide me once he found out I was born in Africa. I believe that was because Thierry was a foreign national as well. He could relate to how much international students strove for a better life in America. Thierry took me under his wing and became like a mentor to me, telling me about the resources available to single moms on welfare like myself.

In addition, he kept directing me to take suitable classes to help me graduate on time to transfer to a California State University, even though attending a university was not on my radar. He continued to mention that going further in higher learning was essential in this world. Although I excelled in his class and school, my free time was still consumed by my bad habits like marijuana, cigarettes, and drinking. Yet, none of that stopped me from attending classes or working. I took some of my classes at night, some at the Chino or Fontana campus. It was not easy, but I was determined not to drop out of school again. I did whatever it took because I had to see it through for my benefit and because, at age thirty-three, I had nothing to show for my existence and I wanted a purpose in life. As I progressed in school and at Fantastic Sams, I was able to rent a two-bedroom apartment, just down the street from my parents' home.

With my part-time job at Fantastic Sams, I maintained a comfortable life with my financial aid, CalWorks money, and food stamps. Tutu, who was now ten years old, had a room at my apartment whenever she visited. Things were good until October 2009. It was time to renew my cosmetology license or else I wouldn't be able to work. Back in 2006, when I opened Tu Studio Hair Designs, a Board of Barbering and Cosmetology agent had visited my establishment to inspect my facility. This inspection turned out to be a prime example of why I had no business opening a beauty salon with no entrepreneurial experience or business knowledge. She walked into my salon. I was working on a client; the other hairstylist there, who was non-licensed, was not working on anyone. She flashed her badge in my face, stating she was from the Board, and inspected my establishment.

I had an out-of-body experience, sweating under my clothes and shaking so much I almost burned the client whose hair I was curling. It was my first time dealing with this, and I had heard not-so-good things about when they visited your establishment. This lady was mean and direct, and with no hint of pity, she told me to keep working on my client as she went into my backroom. She opened cabinets, took pictures for proof, and asked me at one point if the non-licensed hairstylist worked on clients. Thank God he said "no." That would have been another extra $1,000 fine added to the already $995 fine imposed for incorrectly labeling containers and improperly cleaning my tools and the salon. Being an irresponsible business owner, I neglected to pay the fine, which the State Board did not pursue...until the time came to renew my license. Fantastic Sams reminds all their employees a month before a renewal is due because an updated one is always required to stay on the job. I attempted the renewal process online, and I noticed they added the $995 to my $50 renewal fee.

I now needed $1,045 to get my cosmetology license renewed. Mind you, I was still making part-time income and receiving welfare. I had no budget for new expenses and I didn't have an emergency fund. I didn't even know the meaning of an emergency fund at that time. I had no other option but to take a leave from work until I could come up with the money to renew my license.

On November 30, 2009, Fantastic Sams let me go until the Board reinstated my cosmetology license. I left heartbroken, depressed, and mad at myself for being so irresponsible. I sat in the back of the bus that day and cried my eyeballs out. Of course, I had to be discreet about it because I didn't want other passengers to notice me having a meltdown. How would I take care of my bills and pay for my license renewal? It was the only question on my mind. Finally, I had no other option. There was only one thing to do to earn that money. I had but to go back to the strip club. And the sad part of this all was I still had no car to drive to Hawthorne. I didn't care how I got to the club, but I was not about to become homeless again or be forced to live with my parents. As the years have gone by and I reflect on my life, I realize it was all my doing. I was holding myself back. I was standing in my own way.

While I was back physically at the club, my mind and soul were not. After a two-plus-hour commute, I would get there and drink my worries away. This time around, I was desperate to make money to keep my apartment and bills paid. The housing market or financial crises was still looming. Not many decent men came into the club, making my commute worthless because I often returned home with not much after paying the club expenses. All the same, I continued to go.

One day, I was beyond tipsy or high from weed, and it was my turn to go up on stage. The DJ announced, "Up next on stage is *Rasta*!"

On this particular day, the club was packed, and the men were sitting around the stage; they all had their drinks, and everyone seemed to be having a good time. I strutted onto the stage and worked it. Tips were coming at me left and right. There was one gentleman in his late forties who was so into me. He made himself obvious not to miss.

After my performance, I exited the stage and walked around, thanking all the men who had tipped me. By this time, my tall admirer, who was about six foot two, was sitting at the bar waiting for me.

I approached him, looked into those gorgeous green eyes and said, "Thank you."

"You're welcome," he said with a smile in his voice.

I asked him his name, and he said Mark, and asked me to join him.

He bought me a drink and wanted to know all about me. But I had so much stress going on in my life that I just wanted to hurry and give him a couple of lap dances and move on to the next guy.

"So, do you want a lap dance?"

"No, I just want to talk."

I started getting agitated with him. "If you did not want a dance, why are you even at a strip club?"

"Oh, I'm just waiting for traffic to die down before heading home. I live in the mountains and I'm just out here for a contract."

"Ok, well, I have to go get ready for my next set. It was nice to meet you, though."

As I was getting ready to leave he said, "Oh, um. would you like to see me outside the club?"

"What do you mean?" I asked.

"Like out on a date."

It took me back to my North Dakota dancing days when I would go out with Michael. I told him I live in the Inland Empire area, and that's when he said he lived in San Bernardino County. By then, I was in a rush to go get ready.

"Hey, the next time you come in, I'll have an answer for you."

"There's not going to be a next time," he said as he stood up and reached in his wallet. He took out a business card and money. He handed me the card and put the cash on my panty strap on my hip. The club was very dark, so I could not see how much he had tipped me.

"Well, it's going to be your loss if you don't come back in and see me." I smiled.

He laughed. "I'll take my chances."

I hugged him and said my goodbyes. I then headed toward the dancer's backroom to change, but made a quick pitstop out to the back patio designated for smoking and counted what he had tipped me. I was shocked!

Mark had tipped me $1,000! I sat there in disbelief because no man had ever tipped me that much inside Henry King VIII without wanting something, at least a dance in return. I always had to work extra hard to make that much in one day. Smoking slowly on the weed, I pulled out his card and looked at it. He had his own engineering company. I was dazed because this man had just paid off the fine for my cosmetology license without even knowing it. I was over the moon with excitement. Going back onstage, knowing the type of man I had just met, I exuberantly danced my way throughout the night, and felt like a million bucks. Whatever else I made at the club was to pay my rent, on which I was already two months behind. I spent the night at a friend's place and took the train back to Fontana that Sunday morning with a little more than $1,600 in my bag. On that train ride home, I kept thanking God for sending Mark to the club that night. I truly believe that God wanted me to stay out of the strip club because why else would he send someone to give me the actual money needed to reinstate my license? Yes, as a stripper, I did believe in God, and I felt his presence all around me because there had been many times that I woke up in my bed not knowing how I got there. It had to be God looking out for me.

I arrived at the Fontana train station, took a taxi to my apartment, and slept most of that Sunday. I woke up the next morning and went to class. After class, I proudly mailed the money I owed to the Board of Barber and Cosmetology. That was money well spent. I was never returning to King Henry VIII again. And to ensure I never stepped foot in the club, I gathered all my dancing clothes and shoes—and the suitcase—and tossed them into the dumpster. Now, it was a waiting game for my cosmetology license to arrive. Meanwhile I had to figure out how to overturn my eviction notice I received for my apartment. I went to the management office to explain my situation and the reason for my rent being late. But they didn't care about my reasons. They did, however, agree to work with me by allowing me to make payments until I could pay off the amount in full. Things were hard for me! I was still on CalWorks and food stamps but could hardly cover my rent and utilities. I learned that there was a County program call 211 that I qualified for because I was on welfare. Through 211 I was able to get my electricity bill paid for three months. But I still was not catching up on bills fast enough. I was still two months behind on my rent. I had no one to turn to and my survival instincts kicked in. I decided to call Mark, the big tipper from the club. My plan was to be upfront with him, explain my situation and see if he could get me out of the mess that I had created for myself. If he couldn't help me, I would have to deal with the eviction. As I dialed the number on his business card, I had no idea what was coming.

It was January 2010 so a couple months had passed. Once he answered I blurted out, "Hey, so do you still want to take me out on a date?"

I guess he recognized my voice because he said, "Of course!"

He explained that he was out of town on a business trip, but when he got back, we could go out. I said okay. Stressing that it was not soon enough, I cried endlessly in my apartment and prayed for God's mercy. Mark called me on February 13, asking for my home address. At first, I was hesitant because the last time I saw him was three months prior in the strip club. He then asked, "Would you be my Valentine?" I was dumbfounded. This man met me as a stripper. I started thinking he must be pretty lonely if he wanted me to be his Valentine. And since I wanted his help, I did not hesitate. I said, "Yes."

On February 14, before noon, Mark was ringing my doorbell with two dozen red roses in hand. I was totally surprised and impressed. Still battling low self-esteem, I didn't think I deserved the flowers or a man like Mark. He was too kind. Not only did he bring roses, but he brought the food for dinner, wine, weed, and his charm. Mark was the first man to celebrate Valentine's Day with me. *How is it even possible for a former dancer like myself to meet someone like him?*

Still, that February 2010 Valentine's Day was an unforgettable day that I will forever cherish. I have yet to meet a man who can top that day. After spending that night with Mark, I could not bring myself to ask for my due rent. He genuinely liked me and I was digging him too. It became clear that I liked him too much for him to be a sugar daddy. Mark and I started dating.

After the first few dates, I had received my W2, filed my taxes, and was able to use my return to pay off what I owed on back rent. I also received my renewed cosmetology license in the mail and returned to Fantastic Sams, where I excelled and became the top retail seller. I was also passing all of my classes and Mark and I were seriously dating. However, I was still on the bus and taking two buses to work and school was starting to get to me. So I requested to be transferred to the Fantastic Sams near my home in Fontana. But because I was one of the top retail sales and services producers, they didn't want me to leave. My manager was a real…you fill in the blank. Angry and exhausted, I gave my two weeks' notice. Take note: don't ever quit a job without having another one lined up. I left Fantastic Sams in October of 2010 and thank God for my financial aid or else I would have been in the same predicament again. But I landed a job at JCPenney in December. Mark and I continued dating until he mentioned us getting married. That's when I started to freak out. I didn't know how my daughter would take her mom marrying a white man. I became distant from Mark because I was more worried about what people would think or say. There was a period when I cared so much about what others thought of me. And this period was one of them.

It was during this time that my parents received an invitation to a Christmas party organized by the UBSL Association, an organization for the Sierra Leonean community. I decided it would be nice to attend something different and mingle with the African community or, better yet, the Sierra Leonean community. On December 20, 2010, I met Augustine Max Browne, the man who would become my husband four months later. After meeting Max, I called Mark and ended our relationship by telling him it wouldn't work between us because of the way we met, which I knew was a blatant lie. Mark treated me the way a man should treat the woman he adores. He spoiled me, respected me, and the sex was out of this world. But I messed it up. To this day, I regret that I ended our relationship; even more so after realizing that I left him for Max. For the most part, I don't regret my past. There were good days that gave me happiness; the bad days that gave me experiences and lessons. But, one of my biggest regrets is breaking up with Mark. He was a blessing in my life that I didn't see when we were together. I pray to God that He would allow me to know love and recognize it the next time.

Chapter 17
BECOMING A WIFE

―――・・◆・・―――

"Every day you must unlearn the ways that hold you back. You must rid yourself of negativity so you can learn to fly."

- LEON BROWN

When Max and I met at the Christmas party, he approached me with a confident and sexy swagger that I found attractive. He was both charming and well-mannered. At 5'9" with a chiseled body, I could tell he was a regular at the gym. We ended up talking a lot, and I learned he was born in Freetown, Sierra Leone and was one year younger than me. He was Creole, and the only male child among his siblings so he was responsible for providing for his parents back home. Surprisingly, even though I was wearing a custom made, African print dress, he thought I was an American. In fact, he thought I was lying when I said I was from Africa. I had to speak in my native Mende language before he believed me. We talked, laughed, and danced, and by the end of the night he gave me his phone number.

A week or so later, the association had another party for New Year's Eve. My parents and I attended, and I met up with Max. He asked me why I hadn't called him. I told him I usually don't talk to African men because of my experiences with Bobby and Solo. So he insisted I give him my number this time. He called me the next day and asked if we could meet up. I didn't know him that well but still invited him to my place. After Max visited, we started spending a lot of time together and became intimate. Let's just say Mark was a hard act to follow.

Max was sweet, though. I had learned that he had come to America in November of that year to bring his nephew over because his nephew was not old enough to fly by himself. The United States Embassy had given him a visiting visa, and unfortunately, the visa was due to expire in May 2011.

"I do not want to go back to Africa," he said with a sadness in his eyes. "The opportunities are here in America."

"But there's no way you can stay here if your visa expires," I explained.

"I know. That's why I'm looking for someone to marry so I can stay."

One thing I can say is that Max was honest with me from day one. He didn't sugarcoat anything.

I took a deep breath and said, "I don't think I could marry you. I've never been married, and when I do get married, it would have to be for real and not for a visa."

We left it at that.

As the weeks went on and we spent more time together, I began to fall deeper for him, and I felt pity for the guy because all he talked about was not wanting to go back to Africa. Being a Cancer with a sympathetic heart, I started thinking more with my heart instead of my head and essentially settled for him. My reasoning was always: *You're an ex-stripper, Tu. So who would want to marry you?* A woman taking off her clothes for money is not a respectable woman in African culture. Americans might be more forgiving of my past as a stripper. I mean, Mark, who had met me in the strip club would have popped the question if I let him. But

I didn't give him the chance to ask. Yes, I sabotaged a real relationship because I was more worried about what people would say. In hindsight, I never really truly loved myself. So, I settled for Max. Everything about our relationship happened so fast. We met in December and he had moved into my apartment by February, just two months later.

He started saying all the right things a woman wants to hear. I was approaching my thirty-third birthday and coming into that time in life when I felt I was supposed to be married. After all I had been through, I wanted to change my life and build a solid relationship. So when he asked me to marry him, I said yes.

Looking back, what a joke that was. I was getting married for all the wrong reasons, to the point where it looked like I was desperate. I even bought my own engagement ring and wedding bands for us. Granted, I used my JCPenney's Associate discount, but I still bought our rings. If that doesn't scream desperate, I don't know what does.

He was getting married to stay in the country. And honestly, I had my own selfish reasons for wanting to marry Max. First, changing my last name from Carew was very important. That last name belonged to my sisters (or rather my half-sisters, though I have never considered them as such). We have the same mom and were born from the same womb, which should have strengthened our bonds, but my older sister, Sarah, always found a way to remind me we had different fathers, which was unnecessary. I already knew my last name was Kallon. As kids, every time we would fight, Sarah would point out that her sister was Susan (because they shared the same father). I don't know if she understood how that made me feel, and how hurtful it was to hear her say those things to me. So when I met Max, I couldn't wait to get married, to change my last name to Browne.

A second reason for getting married was I thought it would keep me grounded and eliminate any thoughts of ever attempting to go back to my stripping lifestyle. I mean, I had thrown away my dancing suitcase so in all likelihood I was not going back. But getting married would definitely seal that chapter of my life. A married African woman would never be seen in a strip club, or any club for that matter. Of course, these weren't good reasons to get married.

My mom was against the idea of me marrying Max. She told me to my face that Max was using me.

"Why would you do this to yourself and settle for him?" she asked. "This man does not love you. He wants his paper. Once he gets the paper, he will leave you."

But, I never told my mom my reasons for getting married. Instead, I begged my parents to please help me help him by allowing us to move in with them to save money to pay for his immigration paperwork. My parents agreed; they allowed me to bring a man into their house just three months after meeting him. I gave up my Village Drive apartment, and Max and I moved into my parents' home.

I was working part-time at JCPenney and still attending Chaffey College. Unfortunately, Max didn't have a job because of his immigration status. My JCPenney job funded most of his immigration paperwork so he could stay in the United States. After moving in with my parents, Max became a father figure to Tutu. They became close and she liked him, which was huge as she was a teenager at the time. But my parents, on the other hand, were not quite enamored by Max. There were many arguments between me, my parents, and my fiancé.

Yet, against my better judgment and my mother's advice, I married Max on April 6, 2011, with my parents, daughter, and a few of his friends and family serving as witnesses at the San Bernardino County Hall of Records. I was thrilled to become a wife. It was my first marriage, which was supposed to last forever, in my book. I went all out for my dress and ordered the best white African lace fabric from a boutique in Maryland. My gown was custom made for me by an African tailor in San Bernardino. After the ceremony we had a little gathering at my parents' house and invited some of the people from the association. We took photos, of course, but it was important do so to prove to immigration that the marriage was real.

In May 2011, we submitted his immigration paperwork to petition for his work permit in the United States. Within six months, Max received a work permit, and then we got him a Social Security number and California ID.

A month later, we moved into a townhouse in Rialto and shared the rent cost with his family members. Max got a sales job at a car dealership and our lives were stable for a while.

In 2012, I filed our taxes and claimed him as a dependent, giving us enough of a refund to buy our first car together—a 1996 Hyundai Elantra. I finally stopped taking the bus to both Chaffey College and JCPenney.

We shared the townhouse for a while, and before the lease was up for renewal, we decided it was best to move into our own place. The Westcourt Apartments in the city of Colton was the place we called home. It was a roach-infested complex, but it was what we could afford at the time. After moving into our apartment, I decided to improve my credit. I was married and wanted a new beginning. Unfortunately, I had accumulated debt after having to close down Tu Studio Hair Designs in 2008. In addition, I still had the judgment from Charlie's wife.

A co-worker at JCPenney introduced me to a paralegal who could fill out the application and prepare documents necessary for me to be able to file a Chapter 7 bankruptcy at a very reasonable cost. I couldn't wait to get rid of my debt. It would all be one, except for my student loans. At the time, I had nothing to lose. Because we shared a bank account, I told Max. Even though he didn't understand how it worked, he agreed for me to go ahead and do it. In July 2012, I filed a Chapter 7 bankruptcy with the United States Bankruptcy Court Central District of California.

I chose my birthday to file because I consider that date a rebirth—wiping off my debts and starting fresh. What I didn't quite realize at the time was that filing for bankruptcy eliminates your debts, but it also eliminates your access to capital for ten years. It's like you become a financial disease that nobody wants to touch, much less help. It hampers you from getting business or personal loans. Even angel investors will not give you a second thought if you don't have collateral.

The same goes for family members. Knowing that you've filed for bankruptcy, they will have major doubts when it comes to lending you money. Needless to say, declaring bankruptcy would end up being significant hurdle for me down the line.

But on December 10, 2012, when a judge granted the discharge of all my debt under section 727 of title 11, United States Code I was happy and felt a sense of relief. I was no longer saddled by debt.

In my personal life, with Max, things were also getting better. Our lives as we had envisioned were starting to take form.

That is until early 2013 when Max lost his job as a car salesman. This loss took a toll as we started to fight over money. Sometimes we'd go days without speaking to each other. To make matters worse, I received a 50% pay cut from $16 to just $8 per hour because the new JCPenney CEO saw fit to do so. Our fights became nonstop. Max was able to get a security job, and he started making more money than me because he was putting in overtime. Our fights about money increased even more.

He kept telling me, "It seems like you married me so I could provide for you."

I laughed. It wasn't like he was a millionaire when I married him. But money was just one of our problems. Adultery played a huge part as well. One day, we attended an African party, which was frequent because my Sierra Leonean people often do house parties. And sometimes, you don't even need to get an invite; as long as a close friend knows, you will learn about it and invite yourself. I noticed a woman showing too much interest in Max at one of these parties. She tried to get Max's attention by wanting to dance with him. And I even caught them having a conversation at one point. I confronted Max, and he denied that anything was happening between them. So, I dropped it because I had no proof. He maintained his innocence but she is the same woman he is with today.

Another thing that caused us to argue was that I was getting an education. He would complain that it was all about school with me, and that I should quit to find a job to help him pay the bills. What kind of husband would ask his wife to stop going to school? But of course, I refused to leave school; I was just months away from graduating with my associate's degree. I would remind him that my job at JCPenney had provided him with a work permit and that he was being very selfish to ask me to quit school.

Although his tune changed to hoping I would find a better job once I graduated from Chaffey College, we became distant. It was like we were roommates. Some days, he spoke to me; some days, he didn't. I had given up weed and cigarette smoking when we got married. But now, I started drinking heavily. I was drinking my sorrows away while he was drifting away from me. He started spending more time with his friends, attending parties and coming home late at night, which further aroused suspicion that he was seeing someone. I was pretty sure he was having an affair as he suddenly would step outside on our patio to answer his phone calls. But I was in denial because I didn't want to imagine Max cheating on me.

To make matters worse, he began listening to the gossip about my days as an exotic dancer and what strippers do in the clubs to make money. When we met, I told him I was an ex-dancer, but God knows what foul things his friends were saying about dancers. All I know is his behavior towards me was bordering on disgust. My way of dealing with our marriage falling apart was drinking. It became so bad I made a fool of myself one day when our family, including my parents, attended another African party. I drank so much that I blacked out. The next day, my mom told me that she was ashamed of me because of my disrespectful behavior towards them at the party.

In addition, Max took pictures of what I looked like, lying in my vomit and feces all over our bathroom. That will forever represent my most embarrassing, shameful moment. And Max had the evidence, the disgusting photos that I wished would somehow disappear. That was wishful thinking on my part. He continued to talk about or show me those pictures every time he felt like it.

I knew I needed help dealing with his emotional abuse and our rocky marriage, but I didn't ask for it. I had nobody to talk to and I wasn't going to tell my parents for them to say we told you so. So I would go to school like nothing was wrong, but I was hurting inside. The pain of betrayal was unimaginable. I desperately needed an escape and I found one in the form of yoga. Taking yoga classes on campus became my saving grace. I looked forward to my Monday and Wednesday yoga classes which focused on breathing and meditation exercises. Yoga was my introduction to a healthier lifestyle.

I stopped drinking and turned my attention to graduating from Chaffey College. Max started going out clubbing and not spending any more time at home. We were like strangers in our apartment. Our only excitement that year was when I graduated from Chaffey on May 26, 2013. We held a party two weeks later at my parents' house. Celebrating my accomplishment was a wonderful experience. I achieved something—a college degree. But the biggest shocker was yet to come. Right after, I started feeling sick, and was throwing up.

At first, I thought it was because I was hungover from my graduation party, which was the first time I had drank in months. But after I kept throwing up three days later, I realized it wasn't the drinking. So I went to the clinic and blood tests revealed I was pregnant. Before I found out about the baby, Max's mother had constantly asked me when I would have a child.

"You've been married for two years," she said.

"I'm not God," I told myself. *"God is the only one who gives children."*

Early in our marriage, before the fights, we had been trying, but nothing was happening. I wasn't conceiving. The way his mother was talking, I thought Max wanted children. So when the doctor told me I was eight weeks pregnant, I was beaming with excitement. But Max's demeanor completely changed.

Why did he change? I wondered.

When my oldest daughter was born, my mom took care of her. So I thought, here at the age of thirty-four, I would get the opportunity to be a mom again, and this time, be a hands-on mom. I was over the moon with joy to have my baby.

When we left the clinic, I asked him, "Why are you so sad?"

"How can we afford to have a child at this time?" Max asked.

"What do you mean?"

"Our paychecks cannot support the baby and us."

He then had the nerve to ask me to abort our baby. My body went numb. I could not believe this was coming out his mouth. He was telling me to kill our child.

After that, our relationship became even more challenging. Max was suddenly irritated with me for everything I did. For example, one morning, I woke up and went on my knees and started to pray. Max yelled at me, "Why do you have to pray out loud?"

I had prayed numerous times before and during our marriage. Now he was becoming this demonic person that I was not recognizing. I responded to his question by telling him that God was and is still everything to me.

"I put him first before I do anything so you better get used to me praying or the marriage will not work," I said.

The floodgate of tears opened and I was a wreck. I didn't see us as husband and wife. So finally, I asked him between sniffles, "Do you want to separate? I can't continue to live this way. I don't want to be stressed out. I don't want to lose this baby."

"I already told you to get rid of it. So why do you even think I want to be a part of it?" Max responded.

"If you're not happy and I'm not happy, we can give up this lease and go our separate ways," I told him.

He said he wanted me in his life still but didn't want the baby. So he suggested moving back to my parents' house, and we could try to work things out. Like a fool, I believed him. I thought that if we did that, we wouldn't have as many financial issues, and we wouldn't fight so much about money. So I asked my parents, and again, they opened their house to us, and we went back in September 2013 when our apartment lease was up. At my parents' house, Max became even more unbearable. He would go to work, come home, and get dressed up to go out. Finally, my parents started to notice. My mom would ask me if everything was okay. I would lie and say yes. But she knew better. She would see Max come home with shopping bags and leave the house to go clubbing every weekend.

The relationship saving that I thought we were going to do was not happening. There was no more joy in my life. I was four months pregnant and my oldest daughter would look at me sadly as if to say, "Mom, why are you letting him do this to you? Why are you letting him disrespect you and mistreat you this way?"

She was old enough to understand what was going on. At this point, I had lost my self-respect and my dignity was all but gone. I had allowed Max to break my heart, and even damage my pride in front of my teenaged daughter. That was it. That was when I decided enough was enough. I would no longer give him the power to break my spirit. I had devalued myself for far too long, and it was time to stop trying to fix a marriage that was over. The last straw came when I needed gas money to go to work.

"Can I get ten dollars for gas?" I asked him.

"I don't have money," he replied.

He then asked me to drive him to the Enterprise Rent-a-Car place to rent a car to go to San Diego for the weekend.

"Max, I just asked you for ten bucks, and you said you don't have the money, and yet you're going to rent a car to go to San Diego? I need to go to work to provide for our unborn child."

"I told you to get rid of it. I told you I wasn't ready for a baby. That's your problem. I'm going to San Diego to enjoy myself. I didn't come to America for you to trap me in a marriage."

Furious, I left and went to work on an almost-empty gas tank. I was upset the entire time at work. Luckily I was able to make enough tips to put gas in the car. When I got home, I decided it was time to regain control of my life. I packed up everything that belonged to him, put them in the trunk of our car, and drove to his nephew's dad's house in Riverside. I placed it all by the front door, rang the doorbell, and left.

He later called me and said, "You left my stuff in front of a doorway?"

"You don't want me, and that's where your stuff belongs. Why should you continue to disrespect me in front of my daughter and my parents in my family's house? I don't need you. I will take care of my children by myself."

"If you put me out, I'm not coming back."

"That's fine with me," I told him. "You and the woman you're going to San Diego with can go to hell."

"You're not going to make it without me," he said.

"Watch me!" I shouted. "I came to America long before you did. I've made it before and I'm going to make it without you. I will be fine!"

During that first year being separated from him, I hurt so much I thought I might die. It was as if Max had ripped my heart out of my chest, leaving a hole so deep and dark that I didn't have words to describe my pain. Through all the hurt and heartache I finally realized it was time to let Max go. I needed a different type of commitment in my life.

Chapter 18
Finding God

"In God, I move and breathe and have my being"
- OPRAH WINFREY

My parents introduced me to the Church of Jesus Christ of Latter-day Saints when they got baptized. They saw I was struggling with everything in my life. My mom told me being part of something greater than myself might bring me a sense of belonging, so several months before I decided to leave Max I reached out to the missionaries at the church. Two young ladies came over to the apartment. When the missionaries showed up, Max darted into our bedroom and stayed in the room the entire time I held the Bible study. The missionaries came over weekly to teach me the scriptures. If Max was home during their visits, he would stay in the bedroom and once they left, he would find a reason for another argument. He thought I wanted to force religion or the church on him.

"I'm not doing this for you. I am doing this for me," I would say.

"Whatever," he replied. He was still irritated by me inviting the missionaries into our home.

Nonetheless, I continued going to church. Finally, in July 2013 I got baptized a few days after my thirty-third birthday. I felt reborn. Once I got baptized, things changed for me. There was no more drinking. Everything was now about God. I was leading the life I wanted to live. But even though I had found God and now had a personal relationship with Him, I cried a lot. I was five months pregnant then, and my hormones and emotions were all over the place, as you can imagine. One day, one of my mom's friends came to visit. She and my mom decided it was time to talk to me. My mom had given her the update about how I often cried myself to sleep.

"Why do you keep crying over Max?" she asked. "If you should cry for anyone, it should be to God. He's the one who provides for you, gives you life. Max is a mere human. He doesn't deserve your tears. Instead, you should lift yourself up, give God the glory and take care of that child inside you. God will provide for you and your children."

My mom chimed in and said I should keep Max out of my life. "Pull yourself up," she said. "Stop crying. Go back to school and get your bachelor's degree. A man will come in and out of your life, but your education will be in your life forever."

Tears streamed down my face and I was on the verge of sobbing.

"All you need to do now is keep reading your Bible and take yourself back to school," my mom said again.

Interestingly enough, my mom never attended college, but she's extremely savvy when running a business and dealing with money. And she is constantly pushing my sisters and me to go as far as we can in our education.

When I graduated from Chaffey, I wasn't thinking of returning to school. In the back of my mind, I thought I would get my associate's degree and then get a job. That was it. So I asked them both how on earth could I go back to school. I mean, I was almost six months pregnant. They both got on my case. My mom said the best revenge is to succeed in life. She encouraged me to leave everything to God and focus on improving my life for my children. With that said, I was going back to school!

Chapter 19
Getting Back Up

"Our greatest weakness lies in giving up."
- THOMAS A. EDISON

Overnight I became this goal-oriented woman who refused to give up. I reached out to Thierry Brusselle, my professor at Chaffey College. In the email, I pointed out what he had said to me when I graduated with my associate's degree. He said that when I graduate, continuing to my bachelor's was the best way to have a good life. So here I was in his inbox, asking, "Will you direct me to a good college?"

He responded to my email by asking me to come to his office for a meeting to help me figure out the colleges that would be the best for me. He showed me various other colleges and told me why I should choose Cal State San Bernardino (CSUSB). He shared a number of resources available to help me as a soon-to-be single mother again. Then he reviewed the classes I needed to transfer to the university. I hadn't ever thought about continuing my education, so there were some classes I still needed to take at the community college beforehand. One of those was either statistics or mathematics. I'm not a fan of either of those classes. They are hard!

"Oh my goodness," I told him. "Are you sure I need to take math?"

"Don't take my word for it," he said. "Talk to a counselor at Cal State."

I thanked him for his help and left his office hopeful and determined. I called Cal State San Bernardino and set up an appointment with a counselor. Unfortunately, I had missed the application deadline to attend that fall. But that was fine because I still needed to take one of the classes to get into CSUSB.

I found out that Chaffey College was offering a statistics course—and it was a six-week fast-track class in the winter. It was exactly what I needed. At seven months pregnant, an accelerated course was perfect.

My statistics instructor, Professor Gupta, was the most mild-mannered professor.

I told him point blank, "I'm so scared to take this class, but I need it to get into Cal State San Bernardino."

"Don't worry," he said. "You'll make it. You've just got to do class assignments, do not miss class, and you will pass the course."

That's what I needed to hear. The class ran from October through December. It was a night class that met from 6:00 to 7:50 p.m. Professor Gupta guided me through it, and I passed with a C, enough to get me into Cal State San Bernardino!

After the holidays, I met with a counselor again to complete my Cal State San Bernardino enrollment requirements. While in the counselor's office, she told me that I could also apply for scholarships. I went home, turned in the applications, and then waited for the school year to start.

That night, as I lay in bed, I turned on YouTube and typed in Joel Osteen. My mom's friend had introduced me to his ministry. She told me once that his sermons would help me get closer to God, which was what I needed most. His messages comforted me throughout my pregnancy. I would listen to his YouTube channel every night while I lay in bed. As I emotionally reacted to his sermons, I would see Ophelia moving and kicking me in my stomach as I lay there. And then, there were days I just cried myself to sleep.

Chapter 20
OPHELIA

------•◆•------

"Everything I am, you helped me be."

- ANONYMOUS

January 7, 2014 started out like a normal day. I went for my usual walk, something I did every morning. I had read somewhere that regular walks help with a safe and easy birth of a child, so I walked religiously for eight months every day. I enjoyed my walks as they became a great way of coping with stress, plus I loved spending more time in nature. Once I got home from my walk, I made breakfast: Eggo waffles, two eggs, and bacon. As soon as I took the last bite, I felt a sharp pain in my lower belly that took my breath away. Having been down this road before I immediately knew it was a contraction. I told my mom what was happening and she asked if I wanted to head to the hospital, but I remembered the experience with my older daughter's birth. I had gone to the hospital on Tuesday and was there for two days before delivering her. I didn't want to do that again. This time, I wanted to wait until I was ready. I kept feeling the searing pain of the contractions like crazy. They would come and go. I dealt with this pain from 10:00 a.m. until 2:30 p.m.—when Tutu told me she needed to go to a basketball game at Grand Terrace High School. Unfortunately, my parents weren't around to drop her off, and we lived in Fontana, nearly 13 miles away.

"I have to be at my game," she said.

"Why is this game so important?" I asked, breathing through the contraction pains.

"I can't miss the game, mom! I have to be there for my team."

"Ok," I told her, "I'll drive you to the game, and then I'll go to the hospital. This baby is coming soon."

Here I was, basically in labor, driving her to the game, holding my stomach, and doing breathing exercises. I dropped her off and headed straight for Arrowhead Regional Medical Center in Colton, where I had received my prenatal care and had registered to deliver my baby.

When I got to the lobby a security guard tried to stop me until he saw my face. "Did anyone come with you?" he asked. I rolled my eyes because at that very moment his question was irrelevant. The pain was intensifying by the second.

I gritted my teeth and asked, "Where…where is labor and delivery?"

"Fourth floor, ma'am."

When I exited the elevator I was shocked to see there was *a line of people waiting. A long line!*

By now I was in severe pain, but the front desk nurse took her own sweet time. She didn't seem to care, even though she saw I was clearly in labor.

Finally she asked, "Sweetie, who's your doctor."

Hell, I didn't know. All I knew in that moment was that I was in agony. They told me they were going to find me a room. In the meanwhile, they put me on a gurney in the corridor. Finally, they found me a room at about 4:30 p.m.

My mom called to check on me because she did not see my car at home. That's when I let her know I was at the hospital and was about to be taken into the delivery room.

"What! Why would you drive yourself to the hospital? God forbid! You could have gotten into an accident or something," she said. "What floor are you on?"

I told her and she said she was on her way.

The doctor got to my room at about 6:00 p.m., and I was fully dilated and ready to give birth! My mom got there just in time to assist me in pushing. She held my hand and gave me strength. It took about three to five pushes, and my Ophelia was born! The doctor handed her to me. I caressed her naked body on my chest. As I counted her fingers and toes, she held onto my pinky finger. From that precious moment I knew that I would be extremely overprotective of her. For two years, I got down on my knees and I prayed for her when I thought I could no longer conceive children. I wanted to experience motherhood again. This time I would be involved all the way.

"Congratulations," my mom said with a wide smile.

"Thank you!"

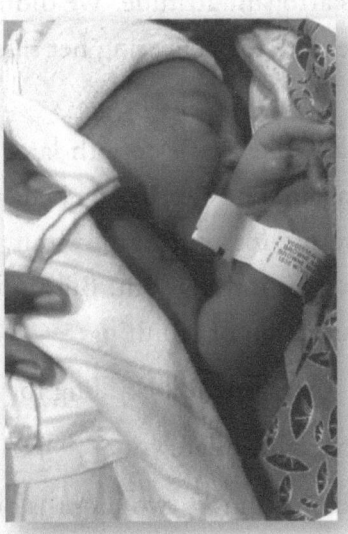

Welcoming Ophelia

Shortly after, the rest of my family arrived, including Tutu. She had told her coach her mother was in labor and about to give birth to her baby sister. He, of course, told her she didn't need to be at the game. So my stepdad picked her up, along with my nephew, and brought them to the hospital.

The next day, Max came to see Ophelia at the hospital. At the sight of him I replayed the last nine months, going through the entire pregnancy alone. I mean, Max would call me now and then, stressing me out. But that was it. I kept my Bible close to me and I also started reading self-help and motivational books like *The Secret* by Rhonda Byrne and *The Seven Spiritual Laws of Success* by Deepak Chopra. I continued to nurture my relationship with God.

But yet, I was struggling with the decision to file for divorce. Even though I had kicked Max out, I didn't want my second child to grow up without a father. I had grown up without a father. My oldest daughter had grown up without her father. I didn't want history to continue to repeat itself. I even asked Max to come back home but he refused.

Now here he stood a day after Ophelia's birth, wearing a designer shirt and carrying this arrogant attitude. We didn't have much to say to each other. He thanked me for delivering her safely and kept staring at our newborn.

The next time he saw her was a month later when he came to my parents' house. Once again, not wanting Ophelia to be without her dad, I asked him to forgive me for putting him out, and I begged him to stay and for us to try to work things out. But unfortunately, he was too prideful. He had no intention of reuniting.

"You know what? That's fine. I'll be filing for divorce."

He laughed. "Yeah, right. I dare you."

Ha! When Ophelia was almost two months old, I drove to San Bernardino County Courthouse and submitted my petition for divorce.

Chapter 21
My Golden Ticket

"I never dreamed of success. I worked for it."
- ESTÉE LAUDER

On July 15, 2015, the judge granted my divorce. My birthday was nine days earlier and this was my best birthday gift ever. I was a thirty-eight-year-old embarking on a journey of cleaning my life of toxins. I wanted everything in my life to be non-toxic. But I was still dealing with my ex-husband for child support. Every time we went to divorce court, Max threw a curveball. He wanted a DNA test to prove that Ophelia was his. In my opinion he was trying to be devious. The court said I didn't need to agree to the test since we were married when we conceived Ophelia, the baby was his regardless. But I wanted the test ordered. Max was very involved with the African community, and they filled him up with so much negative stuff that I agreed to the test. I wanted him to *know* without a doubt that he was the father. I also wanted to prove that I was a faithful wife during our marriage. The results, of course, proved he was the father. But every time we went to court, he wanted something else. After the DNA test, he told the commissioner he planned to return to school to get his GED, but he never did. Then he wanted his child support lowered due to hardship, which the commissioner eventually granted. The support payments dropped from $480 to $350 a month. I remember the day the commissioner reduced Ophelia's child support. Max showed off the pink slip to his new car when we exited the courthouse. He wasn't experiencing any hardship. It hurt me that the court did not see through him and his lies. I vowed never to let him see me broken again. My last words to him in the courthouse parking lot were: "You will see my success." After that, I left everything up to God.

Once the child support case was finalized, I became obsessed with finding my purpose in life and achieving something great. In the process, I embraced me. It was about loving and appreciating everything about myself—my big African nose, my wide smile, and my authentic self—the way God had intended for me to love myself. The mean, negative words Max, my aunt, and others had used to hurt me verbally had evaporated. I decided I would not allow their name-calling to take root in my life anymore. My education would be my golden ticket to finding my purpose. I promised to show up for myself and see my education through to the highest level. I was even more determined when I found one of my old boxes in my parents' garage with my middle school and high school yearbooks. Flipping through the pages I saw I was voted "Most Likely to Succeed" at both schools. It was time to manifest what my classmates had seen in my youth years ago.

My first year at Cal State San Bernardino was among the most rewarding, most exciting times of my life. The Spirit of the Entrepreneur scholarship started me on the path I am on now in my entrepreneurial journey. I was finally working toward something meaningful, allowing me to create a better life for my children and for myself. With my marriage now dissolved, all the toxicity in my life started to take a back seat. I felt liberated, like a new person. I looked forward to going to my classes. College became the place I wanted to be. I cannot explain the emotions, but it felt incredible. The idea behind Tu Organics Salon and Spa actually came to me in an Introduction to Entrepreneurship Venture Capital class. My professor for that class was Mike Stull, the department chair, and the one who had awarded me the Spirit of the Entrepreneur scholarship, so I knew I had to do well in his class. *I told myself I had to pass his class with an A or better. I need to prove I am worthy of the program's scholarship.* So when he told the class to write an essay explaining what we could do that would differentiate us from the rest within our industry, I ran with it. I had been a cosmetologist for nine years and was working as a part-time hairstylist at JCPenney, so I understood the industry, but I never thought of the organic sector for hair. I was in the grocery store's organic section one day when I thought, *Wait a minute; do they make organic hair products?*

The next thing I knew I was googling organic hair salons and hair products. A hair brand called Organic Color System popped up. So there *were* such things as organic hair products. I never thought about something like that. I wrote my essay based on my findings on organic hair products and got an A on the paper. That's when I knew I had found my niche in my industry.

In the following class session, the professor asked an interesting question to those students who had owned a company before: "Would you open another business?"

"I don't think so," I said. "The pain I felt walking away from what I had, I don't want to feel that again. That was a failure."

"It's not a failure," he responded. "It's a lesson learned."

That was the a-ha moment that changed my trajectory. In that instant I realized that I could do it. I could actually start another business. I decided to do it and go all in. I met like-minded individuals like Maritza, Daniel, and Ray, who became my entrepreneur crew. Maritza told me about the Inland Empire Women Business Center and the It's Your Time (IYT) training series it held that helped women kickstart their entrepreneurial ideas. Participants had to complete a business plan with supportive counselors while attending webinars on effective management, marketing, financial projections, and accounting. Maritza had gone through the program and felt I was a perfect candidate for it.

After she explained the advantages of the series, I applied. It turned out Maritza was right. As a recently separated woman with two children, living paycheck to paycheck, working part-time at JCPenney, living with my parents, and on welfare, I fit the whole criteria! That was a blessing. Not that I wanted to be a low-income participant, but it was a blessing I got accepted into the program. My initial investment was $30. I started the ninety-day series alongside many other women who wanted to start or expand their businesses. The center helped me understand the beauty industry through seminars like "The ABCs of Starting Your Own Business" and "Time Management for Entrepreneurs." The program mentored and inspired me every step of my entrepreneurial journey. Through the program, I conducted marketing research on my industry to help create business plans, budgeting, marketing, and creating a vision board through a series of workshops. I would drive 20 miles to Riverside from San Bernardino between classes to attend a workshop, drive back to campus, go to JCPenney, and return home to my almost one-year-old child. I remember one time hitting horrible traffic after attending a workshop. I knew I would be late to my class at Cal State, and this professor was one of those demanding instructors who didn't like his students arriving late. So I emailed him to tell him I was running late and why and asked him to forgive me if I came in late. As I walked into the classroom, my professor put me on blast: "All of you should learn from Tu. She is doing what she must do to make her dreams come true. She is someone you could learn from."

The class clapped for me. I only wanted the professor to understand why I was running late. But, of course, I didn't expect him to do that! But it felt good to get recognition for my hard work. That zeal. That passion.

I don't know where it came from inside me. But I knew I wanted my children, especially my older daughter, Tutu, to see that with dedication and determination, anything is possible. It's not easy but it's possible.

During the IYT program, I hit a roadblock when I got to the financial portion of the business plan. Everything for that financial section I based on JCPenney's hair salon brochures. Since I was working there, it only made sense to use their brochure as a guide. But I didn't know how it would be for an organic hair salon. It wasn't looking right, and I almost gave up.

My mentor, an accountant and business counselor with IEWBC, told me, "Tu, you've come this far. You can't give up. It's the last part of the plan. You can't quit." She laid it on thick: "Do you want your ex-husband to see you as a failure? You're doing this for your kids."

She told me my numbers didn't have to be entirely right; they could be a "guesstimate." However, I had to show something in the financial section to enter the competition. So I submitted the plan the night before the contest was over. I came in second place, surprisingly! That should tell you not to give up. Keep going no matter what!

After completing the IYT program in January 2015, I felt like I was on top of the world; nothing could stop me! So I did the stupidest thing ever: I bought myself a Range Rover. Hear me when I say, please, don't buy a luxury car if you are on welfare or don't have money in the bank for maintenance. I was trying to prove my worth to my ex-husband. But, unfortunately, it's like Dave Ramsey said, "Too many people buy things they don't need with money they don't have to impress people they don't like." Now, as I look back, this quote spoke directly to me. He was the motivation behind my purchasing the Range Rover and everything else I did after our separation. But once our divorce was finalized, that's when it hit me. I had to put myself first. Maya Angelou said it beautifully: "You may encounter many defeats, but you must not be defeated.

In fact, it may be necessary to encounter the defeats, so you can know who you are, what you can rise from, how you can still come out of it." It was not about Max anymore; I had to build a life and a career and become financially stable. I had to go full force or nothing at all. And I did it. It was time to turn my business plan into reality. I would launch my business on my own. This time, no one was giving me anything, like how Charlie bought my first salon. It involves sweat, blood, and energy, but it is more rewarding when you work hard for something. It makes you appreciate it even more. Tu Organics Salon and Spa was my ticket to a life of financial stability. Every school project, especially marketing and management classes, involved my business plan. I always went to my professors and asked if I could use my business for class projects. "As long as your classmates are willing to go along with you, you can," they would say.

Some of my ride-or-die classmates offered support. Daniel designed the Tu Organics logo on a napkin during one of our class sessions. Maritza created the first Tu Organics Salon and Spa T-shirts. And Ray was with me every single step. When we became friends, Daniel had almost completed his MBA, and Maritza was halfway to achieving her bachelor's degree. Because I was pursuing a dual degree, I stayed behind with Ray, who was starting his MBA program. So our friendship grew closer. He supported my class projects and the accolades I received during our time at CSUSB. He would always praise me by saying, "You're going to be so big in your industry." He gave me all the support I needed. On New Year's Eve through January 4, 2018, I fell sick from an ingrown hair on my collarbone, which turned out to be a cyst, resulting in me being admitted to the hospital. Ray not only visited me but showed up with flowers and a card. He always made my day by showing up. Ray would unexpectedly show up at the salon to keep me company and ask about the business. We became the best of friends, and sometimes we would jokingly say, if he were not gay, he would have been my perfect partner. That's how good of a friend he was.

When I found out that he had cancer, I was devastated. He hid his illness for the longest; I eventually found out when he ended up at Loma Linda Hospital. It was my turn to be there for him. Each time I visited him, though, he would say: "Good things are going to happen to you. I see that God is going to bless you." My friend was on his deathbed, still telling me not to give up, motivating me. One of the most memorable and saddest conversations we had was me sitting at his bedside during one of my visits, and he said he didn't think God would accept him into his Kingdom because he was gay. So I would pray for him and read the Bible to him to calm his way of thinking. Before he passed, I reached out to the Childhood Cancer Foundation of Southern California, Inc., based out of Loma Linda, and told them I wanted to do a toy drive in Ray's honor. The first year Ray was still with us, I took the thank you card that the foundation signed to show him at the hospital; he was so pleased and grateful.

"You did this for me?" he asked.

"Yes, and I will continue to do so until Tu Organics Salon and Spa is no more."

I have continued as I had promised him. He was a huge part of my life. It was a massive blow for me when he passed, and I wish he could see how well I'm doing now. But I know that he is watching over me. Friendships like Ray's come once in a lifetime, and I don't take them for granted. I pray he was accepted into God's Kingdom because that is where he belongs.

Chapter 22
Closed Doors

━━━•··◆··•━━━

"God is the primary investor in my business"
- ANONYMOUS

God definitely works in mysterious ways. On September 16, 2016, I left JCPenney, with no plans to ever return. However, I would not have left that department store salon if they had not rejected me for a lead position. The salon leader was going for a job at Sephora, and she told me to apply for her post because I qualified. After all, when I attended Chaffey College, I had a concentration in Management. Encouraged, I took her advice and applied for the position. I thought since I was already working for the company as a hairstylist, there was a strong possibility I would get the lead position. The area manager even made me feel like I would get it. She told the entire salon staff that I would be training for the position, and as I was getting trained, I would be the acting salon lead. All the stylists and I thought I would eventually get the job. Instead, they used me in every way possible by telling me to micro-manage the hairstylists and take care of the salon responsibilities. Six months later, they introduced another lady as our salon leader.

I was shocked, and so was everyone who thought I would be their leader. That was the first time I experienced how corporations only care for themselves. The biggest successes usually come after the biggest frustrations. And let me tell you, I was frustrated with how JCPenney used me. So I decided to turn my frustration into motivation.

I focused on finishing the Inland Empire Women's Business Center training series. With just two weeks left to complete the series, a fellow participant told me about another program that would benefit me—a matched savings incentive program. The Citadel Community Development Corporation funded the grant program, which offered two-to-one match savings for participants interested in purchasing their first home, pursuing an education, or starting or expanding a business. But, of course, participants needed to provide some seed money first. I went to the Community Action Partnership offices in Colton and discovered that I had to be a Riverside County resident to participate. Unfortunately, I was a San Bernardino resident, but I applied anyway. To my surprise, they didn't turn me down!

When I joined the program, they told me I needed to provide $2,000 in seed money, and the program would match me in a 2-to-1 match. I would then have a total of $6,000 to start my business. But, first, I would attend workshops on fixing my credit, writing a business plan, and finances. Because I already had a business plan, the program accepted my business plan workshop as completed. Due to my bankruptcy and poor credit score of about 560, I went to the workshop to build up my credit. Next, the online classes showed me how to budget. As part of the program, they opened up a bank account through Citibank, and I had to deposit $40 a month until I could fund the entire $2,000 seed money. So with every paycheck I got from JCPenney, I would make my deposit and eventually saved $2,360.

Once I completed the program, I had $6,360 waiting for me in a savings account. I then started looking for investors. Note that I had bad credit but a good business plan. So I reached out to anyone who could help me. Cal State's Entrepreneurship Program would hold a "Dinner with an Entrepreneur" event where you could meet and network with businesspeople. I met a man there who told me, "If you show me your business plan, I might be interested in investing."

So, when I completed the Savings Match program, he was the first person I called. But, unfortunately, that call was a huge disappointment. He didn't help me at all. Instead, he sent me to his banker, who told me I had a good plan but couldn't help me.

"Salon businesses are high-risk to loan money to," he said. "They tend to fail easily. Come back in five years and we can help you then."

Seriously? How am I supposed to do that if I have no money to start a business in the first place?

I went to the Inland Empire Women's Business Center for resources, and they referred me to a small bank called ACCION of San Diego, a non-profit organization. It bases its loans on your credit and if you have a job and collateral. John, the loan manager, asked me to email him my business plan.

"You have a wonderful business plan. Organic business is where the future is heading," he said.

I was excited because a banker liked my plan. He said the bank was willing to loan me $15,000 to start a business based on my credit score. I didn't know how much it took to start a business. I was just happy I got some money. I didn't have any collateral, except my Range Rover, which was the biggest mistake of my life. John asked me if I had seed money. I said yes, through Citadel.

So I started to look for a location. But, of course, it is always best to buy an established business rather than start from a new space. When I finally found one, I excitedly told John about it. He asked me about the rent, which $2,800 a month. But unfortunately, the space was empty, so I would need to put in the plumbing, fixtures, etc.

"Oh, we have a problem," he said. "There's no way the bank can give you the money. Because by setting up the space, the money would run out. And you will be done."

I pleaded with him. However, John explained the money wouldn't go far. It just wouldn't work. "Find an established business and call me, and I will reconsider the offer," he said.

I got off the phone disappointed and dejected. Tears were running down my face. My heart felt like it could not take anymore. That was my last hope, and he had just snatched it away. I went to my mom's room and just started sobbing.

"Why are you crying? It's not a crying matter; it's a praying matter," she told me. "Let God handle it."

I remember weeping and walking back to my room overcome by sadness. I didn't know how God was going to help me. I eventually cried myself to sleep. I don't know what woke me up, but at 3:00 a.m., I woke up in the middle of the night, grabbed my Bible, and started praying. I was crying so much my Bible got drenched with my tears. Six years later, when you open my Bible, where I prayed that night, it feels crunchy because of my tears. After praying, I opened up my Mac, logged into Craigslist, and typed "salon for sale in Rancho Cucamonga." *Hair by Megan* came up, and it was for sale!

The salon had six stations, two pedicure chairs, and a facial room. It was 1,080 square feet, almost exactly what I had written in my business plan a year prior (1,000 square feet). I was amazed at how God was so wonderful. I just knew it was God's doing! No one can tell me otherwise!

The following day, I called the owner, Megan, and asked if the salon was still available for sale.

"I didn't know that ad was still up. I posted that six months ago. You're the first person to respond to the ad," she said. "It's still available. When do you want to come to see it?"

"I'll be there tomorrow morning!"

My mom went with me to the salon. It was the ugliest salon I had ever seen. I asked how much she wanted for the business, and she said $18,000. I told her what I could afford. She told me she would speak to her family and then get back to me. She didn't call until a few days later, and during those two few days, I kept checking my cell phone to ensure the volume was on a high and the battery was fully charged. It was the longest three days of my life. Finally, she called and said, "I accept your offer."

"It's a deal!" I was so excited. I then called John to tell him I had found an established business.

"Would you please reconsider giving me a loan?" I practically begged.

He asked for details about the salon. The first thing I said is "It has equipment!"

"That's good," he said. "We can use it as collateral. Is the business willing to give you a profit-loss statement?" he asked.

Megan sent me three years' worth of statements, which I forwarded to John.

"I will do the numbers and get back to you," he said.

It was Labor Day weekend. I took my children to the beach, but I remember laying on sand being worried I would be rejected again for the loan. So, I turned to my God, and I prayed:

Dear God, you are above every area of my life, and it is by your hand that my world is together. If it is your will, pave the way for the bank to approve the business loan. All glory and honor belong to you alone. Take control. In Jesus Christ's name. Amen.

John finally called after the weekend and said, "Guess what I'm going to do for you? I can give you $10,000, the maximum I can give you.

But, first, I have to send one of my employees to take pictures of the equipment we would use for collateral."

"John, the $10,000 is all I need!" I told him. "Thank you for even giving me this opportunity."

Three days after my conversation with John, I drove to ACCION's office in downtown Riverside to sign the loan documents, and the money was made available to buy the business from Megan. I got the loan with a 19% interest rate! Word of advice: don't fuck up your credit. Take it from me. I had a credit score of 560 when I started my business in 2016.

During all of this, as I was trying to get my business up and running, I was still working on my undergrad degree! Whenever I went on campus, I shared my journey with my professors and classmates. Everyone was all excited. It was a great time for me. I needed thirty days before taking over the salon because I had to get things in order with JCPenney. When I put in my two-week notice, I remember telling my manager I had bought a salon. She couldn't believe it.

"Are you sure you're not going to come back in a year or so?" she asked.

"Watch me. I'm not looking back!"

Since I needed extra money, I cashed out my JCPenney 401k, worth $4,000 (another big mistake since I was penalized 10% for taking out the money before I turned fifty-nine). I would never do that again, but it was worth it for my business. As a result, I started my salon for less than $18,000.

On September 29, 2016, I welcomed my first clients, Victoria, Brent, and Mary. They followed me from JCPenney along with seven other loyal clients.

I was on my way, or so I thought. Before completing the sale with Megan, the building manager heard of my bankruptcy and wanted to see my business plan. She also wanted a double deposit because of my poor credit. I know I should have had a lawyer and an accountant, but I couldn't afford either at the time. I signed the lease with the building manager without an attorney present. Everything happened so fast. I signed everything the building manager gave me—not reading the fine print.

My salon's grand opening was fast approaching. I called Citadel, told them about the salon, and asked for the seed money. They wanted to see all the paperwork to make sure it was legitimate, and on August 31, they made a check out to me for $6,360. I used that money to pay for a storefront sign and products and painted the salon. I bootstrapped by using the worn-out equipment that came with the salon, which I eventually changed as I generated cash two years later. I would also slowly change the salon's interior as I had envisioned it in my business plan.

To get the salon ready for the October grand opening, I reached out to members of my church and told them about my business. As a result, I was allowed to go to the podium and make my announcement, asking for help. Four or five church members showed up at the salon and helped paint and clean to ensure everything was ready for the grand opening.

On October 28, 2016, Tu Organics Salon and Spa had its official grand opening. Representatives from the Rancho Cucamonga Chamber of Commerce, which I had joined, attended. So did my classmates, professors, and people from the Inland Empire Women's Business Center. My mom and Ophelia came too. I had all of these people come to support me. It was an amazing day. I remember the salon booth renters saying this was a big deal because the previous owner (absent for the grand opening) didn't renovate the space or have an opening celebration.

Tu Organics Salon and Spa startup products
at hand during Grand Opening in 2016

For my first salon, I didn't do anything of that magnitude either. This time, I was determined to do things differently.

I learned a lot that I applied to this new business. But I encountered hardship a year and a half later when I got scammed out of six thousand dollars by a man I met on a dating app. How did he scam me, you ask? Remember, I told you my credit was terrible? He started by asking me if I had credit cards, and I told him yes, but they are all maxed out because I had been robbing Peter to pay Paul, if you know how that saying goes. So he said, "Oh baby, I want to help your business grow because whatever benefits you benefits me." He offered to pay off two of my credit cards with the most balance. I had my business and personal Capital One credit cards with a three-thousand-dollar balance, plus interest and late fees. He asked me to give him all my card details and said he would take care of everything.

With my naive self, I did. I was like, this man is incredible. So, out of desperation, I gave him my card username and password. The next time he texted me, he said he had paid everything in full. I thought I was the luckiest woman to meet a man like this. Yes, I know what you are thinking. I was one of those women who went on the news to talk about men they met online and got scammed, losing thousands of dollars. The only difference between those women and me was that I kept it to myself because I felt stupid for being taken advantage of and caring for a stranger I had never met. He would always say his job keeps him busy traveling the world, but he couldn't wait to meet me. Again, I was looking for love in all the wrong places. Please don't judge me because I was getting over my divorce, and this was my first time trying to date again. He blinded my common sense with his sweet texts. Five days later, after the money cleared on the credit cards and both showed zero balance, I received a text message in the middle of the night that read, *I need you to Western Union me one thousand dollars.* Then another one until all the money on the card was back where I started. Every time he asked me to send him money, I would say, but I thought you said you were helping me. He would say, "Baby, I promise, don't worry. I will take care of you."

A few weeks in, Capital One contacted me. Basically he left me with my three-thousand-dollar debt, plus an extra three, making it six thousand dollars. The bad part was his profile picture was a Caucasian man, and he turned out to be Nigerian.

How did I find out that he was Nigerian? He had the nerve to call me on my cell phone about six months later. I remember my body going numb. Mind you, we had never spoken before. It was all texted messages for three months before he scammed me. Now, he called me to ask me to forgive him for what he did to me and then told me he lives in Nigeria, like that was supposed to make a difference for what he did to me. I told him God would punish him, and then I hung up the phone. I can now find the courage to talk about it because everyone makes mistakes on their way to success. It's a sign that you are learning and trying new things. Would I use dating apps again? HELL NO! That was an expensive lesson, and it took me years to rebuild my credit score again.

One thing is for sure: I don't need a man to take care of me financially anymore. As far as dating goes, I don't stress the idea anymore. The right man will find me either by me giving him a haircut, at a grocery store or gas station, but it will not be on a dating app. Anyway, the building manager and the owner used this tough time against me by renting the other unit directly adjacent to mine to a direct competitor. When my lawyer responded to what they were doing to me, the landlord responded with a Pay-or-Quit order. It was the worst experience of owning a business. They took advantage of me during my hard times. However, I learned that once you face the darkness, it is easier to walk through the light.

Chapter 23
A Tough Road

───── ·••◆••· ─────

"Whenever you see a successful business, someone once made a courageous decision."

- PETER F. DRUCKER

I knew I would face some obstacles while building my business, but damn! I never anticipated the extent of how tough the road ahead would be. Even though I had a salon, I still needed a second job to pay my household bills. I was adamant about not going back to JCPenney but I needed a job that worked with my schedule. So I started working at UPS as a package handler. I attended my classes at CSUSB in the mornings, went to the salon right after class, then at midnight went to UPS and loaded trucks until 6:00 a.m., and then returned to Ophelia (who was around two years old at the time). I had too much stuff going on, but somehow I made it work. I worked at UPS from November 2016 and quit right before Christmas. Because of the holiday rush, UPS managers were brutal during these times. They wouldn't let me leave to go to my business, and I couldn't ignore my business, so I quit. I was at UPS to make extra income to pay my bills and keep my business doors open, not to be a handler for Jeff Bezos's Amazon packages. No offense to package handlers. It's a respectable job; I just had a business startup to run.

My business, however, was growing slowly. I didn't have a lot of customers after opening my salon at this time—just the ten clients from JCPenney who came with me because of the outstanding hair care service I provided. Plus, I took care of their souls by giving a listening ear to their problems. I was advertising and doing everything I could, but business wasn't picking up. Money was dwindling, bills were piling up, and I needed to find a way to make money fast. The booth rentals helped, but it was not enough. The salon rent at the time was $2,300, so all the money I was bringing in from booth rentals was going to rent. But what about utility bills? I had a display shelf for products, but I didn't have money to buy products to sell. And due to the scam I experienced, the scammer had maxed out my business credit card.

I desperately needed another source of cash so I became an Uber and Lyft driver. Another poor decision! Whenever it was slow at the salon, I would work Uber and Lyft. But that got to me fast. To get decent money I had to drive far, like sixty miles one way to Los Angeles. Not knowing who my passenger was going to be, I felt I was putting my life on the line. Plus I hated being away from my business location in case a client called and wanted service. Also, I had a brand-new car—a Honda Accord (I had traded in the Range Rover) that I was putting a lot of mileage on. Ultimately, I decided it wasn't worth it. I stopped driving for Uber and Lyft.

Megan, whom I had purchased the salon from and who said she would stay on for a year renting a booth ended up only staying for nine months. When she left, that hurt. I needed to replace what she was paying for her booth rental from somewhere else. As a result, I fell two months behind on the salon rent and electricity bill. I felt the pressure of being an entrepreneur but still trusted myself and did my best to remove any doubts appearing in my head.

One day, my mom came to the salon for me to retighten her dreadlocks, and it was good that the booth renters were not working that day;

so it was just the two of us in the salon. She asked how the business was doing and I had no choice but to go there. I told her the sad truth and before I knew it, I was crying. It was the first time she had asked about the company since I opened it. I had never involved my mom or stepfather in my business. She and everyone else thought I was doing well. So when she heard me bawling, she knew it was severe. I explained everything I was doing to keep afloat, but it seemed like I was going nowhere. I then asked her if they could loan me money to pay my salon rent.

"The money I have is not mine alone; ask your stepdad," she said. "I will also speak to him on your behalf."

Asking my stepdad would not be a problem because his usual answer would be, "Whatever your mom says." But I knew my mom wanted me to ask him out of courtesy and respect. My parents ended up loaning me $5,000. I told them I would pay them back every cent. I was able to pay the salon rent for a month and hoped to play catch-up for the rest and buy some products for retail. Also, I became very creative. I would give my clients samples, ask them to pay for their products upfront, and pick them up once their orders arrived at the salon. The first three years of Tu Organics Salon and Spa were the most challenging years of my entrepreneurial journey. I worked over eighty to a hundred hours weekly and did everything myself. I was handling my QuickBooks account, doing marketing, and wearing the management hat too. The sleepless nights were terrifying because I would find myself sitting at the edge of my bed crying.

Ophelia saw me less and less. I would be so exhausted when I got home that I would only check in on Ophelia, who sometimes slept between her grandparents in their room or with her older sister, Tutu. Thank God that I was living with my parents during this period. Because finding a sitter and paying them would have been another expense I could not afford. I struggled with so much self-doubt, but I was determined to overcome and prevail. I had to prove to myself that I could do this. I had no choice anyway; I had to make it; there were no ifs, ands, or buts about it. I did not come this far just to come this far. Life was a struggle, and the only people who knew the truth were my mom and stepdad. And they turned out to be the perfect support system that I needed.

Note that I had earned two bachelor's degrees from CSUSB. However, education had little to do with how I would keep my salon doors open. Instead, it was about grit, determination, and the execution of my ideas.

Chapter 24
Becoming Professor Browne

―――――•◆•―――――

"Be so busy loving your life that you have no time for hate, regrets, or fear."
- KAREN SALMANSOHN

One of the ideas I had was recruiting cosmetology students to work at Tu Organics Salon and Spa. I wanted stylists and cosmetologists who would understand my vision and be willing to learn about my company's culture. That's when a light bulb went on in my head. Becoming a cosmetology instructor would help me reach up-and-coming cosmetologists. Furthermore, the young hairstylists would resonate with an eco-friendly beauty salon.

I reached out to a former Chaffey College classmate via LinkedIn and found out she was an instructor at Riverside Community College (RCC). I explained to her that I needed to work in an environment that would help me hire employees.

"You know RCC has a training program for instructors?" she said. "Once you graduate, you can apply, and they will hire you."

I took her advice and enrolled in the six-month instructor training program. My goal was laser focused: to become an instructor and hire students from RCC to work in the salon, bringing in a new generation that would be more open-minded and willing to embrace organic hair products. It would be a win-win for the students and myself. The students would gain salon experience and mentoring, and I would have help. It was a brilliant idea, I told myself.

However, I also needed to make some extra cash because the holidays were approaching, and I wanted my children to have a good Christmas, especially Ophelia who was now four years old. The guilt of being gone all the time made me feel like a terrible mother. I wanted to give her a memorable Christmas gift, and with the business still struggling, I decided to get a late-night job at FedEx for the holidays. I could put her to bed and then go to work. So I applied and became employed in package handling (the same job I had with UPS). I worked at FedEx from 11:00 p.m. to 6:00 a.m., went to RCC for my instructor training class at 8:00 a.m., and returned to the salon at 3:00 p.m. I was burning myself out, and it started to take a toll on me and my grades at RCC. After I failed an exam, I went to the professor, the dean of the cosmetology department, and told him I would never get a failing grade in his class again.

"What is going on?" he asked.

"I want to pass your class, and I am doing too many things at once. I will get better grades moving forward," I said.

I continued working at FedEx after the holidays because I was so set on making my business survive. But once my grades started to fall, I had to evaluate what was most important to me: making money or bringing students to work at my salon. I decided the salon was my long-term goal and left FedEx.

Once I did that, I paid more attention to the company. I came up with ideas. Then another booth renter decided to leave. She had been with me since I bought the salon from Megan and was the only one using non-organic products. She didn't feel comfortable with that. At this point, I didn't care anymore.

"I think it's for the best," she said.

Now it was just the two nail technicians and me. They had their clientele and did their jobs. I had five stylist stations empty and a facial room not being used. I was not utilizing my beauty salon to its full extent.

So I brought in commission workers—on a fifty-fifty arrangement as I wanted to be fair. For example, they would do a facial for $60—they would get $30, and I would keep the other $30. I was losing money because I provided the products, but I didn't mind because the business was still operating. While the salon started taking shape, my mom decided she wanted to return to work. I was fortunate that my mom had taken care of Ophelia for the past years. But, the selfish part of me said, "No, who's going to watch Ophelia?" But my mom said that we would figure it out. After that, everyone helped to care for Ophelia, including my parents and my oldest daughter. Finally, a couple of church members agreed to watch Ophelia for a reasonable cost. She was either with a church member or my parents, never in daycare. It was tough, but I made it happen.

In June of 2018, I completed the Instructor Training class at RCC and applied for the instructor position right away. With me being overly qualified for the job, they hired me immediately. So, in February 2019, I was a Riverside Community College professor. My path in teaching was rewarding. I provided jobs for some of my students to work at the salon while earning a second steady income stream. But, there were also challenges. I was about two semesters into my teaching career at RCC when I noticed students whispering every time I passed them. For the life of me, I could not figure out why. I later found out that another instructor told some of her students that I used to be a stripper. This particular instructor had sent me a friend request on Facebook, which I accepted because we were colleagues. Also, during this time in my life, I started to share that I was a former dancer and began embracing my past.

I guess after she saw one of my posts, she shared it with her students, which was mean-spirited. But she was known to spread gossip and talk about others in our department. I was furious that she shared my past and wanted to confront her, but I chose to love her instead. Like Mahatma Gandhi said, "Whenever you are confronted with an opponent. Conquer him with love." So I let it go and started incorporating my dancing into my introduction. As I grew in my teaching style at RCC, I would ask my students to introduce themselves and give me a little background about themselves, what brought them to RCC, and where they saw themselves in five years, and I would do the same.

After they all introduced themselves, I would introduce myself, explaining where I came from in Africa. Then, I told them I danced for ten years as a stripper. I went on to say that I had been on welfare and I experienced many difficulties before going back to school and eventually earning my bachelor's and master's degrees. I'd fast forward to the now, standing in front of them as their instructor and a business owner. As I finished introducing myself, to my surprise, all my students stood up and gave me a standing ovation.

That was the first time I understood that any one of us could inspire people or, in my case, my students. It was a decisive moment for me.

But that's not how it began when I first started teaching. I never started my class by introducing myself or telling my students about my past. But, when I found out what the other instructor had done, I figured the students should hear it directly from me.

Initially, I was terrified and apprehensive about how the students would take it. But, I figured these male and female students were in their 20s or at least adult enough to appreciate my honesty and authenticity with them. And once I did, I felt liberated. Sharing my story with them lifted something off my shoulders. I had exuberant confidence! I was no longer scared or worried about what others said behind my back. And at the beginning of every semester, when I introduce myself to my students, one or two students will inevitably pull me aside during break to share their struggles with me. I've had a couple of students tell me they worked as an exotic dancer while attending school.

My childhood molestation, the name calling by my aunt, telling me that I am ugly, my domestic violence experiences, and my ex-husband's infidelity all led me to this path of inspiring others. As a result, my students felt safe sharing their stories with me and it felt good to be there with a listening ear. I was not judging them but relating to them. It also taught me that it is okay to be yourself and go through struggles because it is not where you are; but where you're going. Are you going to continue getting in your way or remove the barriers? Which is it?

Inspiring others became my purpose after getting a standing ovation from my students. How many people can say their professor was an ex-stripper? My students can say that and then further say she earned two bachelor's degrees, an MBA, and owns two beauty salons in two different states, even if one of those salons was inside a shared space. I am a survivor! I have survived molestation, growing up without a dad, and been abused in every way possible, but I still did not become a victim. Instead, I am a victor.

MBA Graduation 2020

When I started as a professor I was focused on building my business, but later I became obsessed with sharing my story and inspiring my students who might go through similar issues and have the potential to come out on top. I prayed for God to use me in any form for me to reach the masses with my message of survival, even as a professor.

Chapter 25
Shining During the Struggle

---•••◆•••---

"Don't judge me by success. Judge me by how many times I fell down and got back up again."

- NELSON MANDELA

I'm not going to sugarcoat it. Even as a professor, the business struggle was real! At this time, I only had a couple of stylists and they were working on commission, but a new law passed that required all stylists to either be on payroll or work as independent contractors. So of course, the stylists left. Who could blame them? Nobody who is making pretty good money even with a 50/50 split is willing to suddenly be making minimum wage. I needed stylists to work in the salon and I needed customers.

When I got a call from an intern with the city of Rancho Cucamonga asking to do a story about my salon, I was surprised and honestly, shocked. I was barely making it, but she wanted to write about my salon. She was looking to recognize green companies in the city. I recycle everything, plus all of my products are plant-based and I use LED lights. I'm all about sustainability. In fact, the city of Rancho Cucamonga recognized my beauty salon as the first green salon in Rancho Cucamonga. I was very proud of that!

On January 12, 2018, the article about my business appeared in the *RC Grapevine* newsletter, a local publication for residents of Rancho Cucamonga. I remember customers coming in because they read the magazine as well as saw a video interview I had done on the local TV channel. It was the recognition I needed as my client list began to increase. It was all God's doing because every day when I entered my salon, I would pray:

Dear God, may my business be a blessing to everyone who works here and everyone it serves. May it both bring and attract prosperity and love.

I had read this prayer in Marianne Williamson's book, *The Gift of Change*. This became my daily prayer for the salon. The recognition and local media attention was the change my business needed for the community to know we were in Rancho Cucamonga. The publication, the video, and the mayor presenting the Certificate of Recognition to me with the participation of the rest of the City Council members were very proud moments. To my surprise, other recognitions followed that year. In April, I was asked to be on a panel for the Inland Prosperity Women's Conference. It was the first time I shared my entrepreneurial journey, which was very nerve-wracking. Tutu sat in the front row. It was the first she was going to hear me speak in public. I wanted her to experience this. After my talk, many women came forward, asking me questions and telling me how inspirational my story was.

It was wonderful to hear people say things like "Your story inspired me to propel forward." I didn't expect a reaction from so many women. I could not believe I had shared a panel with amazing women with so much more going for them than me. Then there was me, someone who was actually still struggling as a small business owner, but inspiring others.

The biggest compliment, though, came from my daughter on the ride home.

"Oh my God, Mom, I didn't know you were awesome! And women were waiting to get a chance to speak with you one-on-one. I am so proud of you, mom," she said.

She was shocked to see me at this level, having people attend a conference to hear me speak. The whole experience was extremely impactful for me. It gave me a different level of confidence. That's when I knew I had the power to make a difference. I left that conference with a burning sensation to share more of my story. I began volunteering to speak more often. I started to become comfortable and confident being a motivational speaker.

In May, Tu Organics Salon and Spa received the Small Business Administration's Micro Business Award. Again, I was blown away. An SBA award? It is something I could not have imagined. I recall Michelle Skiljan from the Inland Empire Women's Business Center introducing me as a "woman who has taken advantage of all the resources available to propel her business forward." It was true; I took the resources available and ran with them! I posted on social media what the award meant to me:

> *Starting this business was all about proving something to my ex-husband. Now it's becoming something bigger than myself. I'm just getting warmed up. What a blessing! I'll continue to inspire women and hopefully make a difference in my little way. Everything I have experienced prepares me for moments like this and what's to come. I am looking forward to hanging this award with my other accomplishments on the salon "Wall of Fame."*

I had no idea I would continue to add to the "Wall of Fame." After all, I was busy averting a crisis that could have ended my business for good. I had a verbal agreement with a young lady I was mentoring. We agreed that she would work in the salon for a year and I would train her.

She would take home whatever she made from her clients. Once the law was passed about stylists being on payroll or working as contractors, I informed her that she could do the latter, but I'd need to charge her booth rent, a standard practice in the industry. The next day she asked to meet with me and during this meeting she said, "Tu, I've been doing some calculations and I believe you owe me $10,000."

My jaw dropped. "What are you talking about?"

Never acknowledging the verbal agreement we had, she explained that over the last year she believed that I owed her. Of course, because nothing was in writing, she had my back against the wall. She threatened to report me to the Cosmetology Board. So we came up with a new agreement (this time in writing) that she would work in the salon for a year, use my products, and not pay booth rent in order to recoup the supposed $10,000 I owed her.

With all that going on, in October the National Association of Women Business Owners/ (NAWBO) Inland Empire Chapter nominated me as one of their Amazing Women 2018 for the "Rising Star" award category. Although I didn't win, I still count as a huge accomplishment to be recognized for someone just getting her business off the ground.

After that I was nominated for the Spirit of the Entrepreneur Award, one of the most prestigious awards in the Inland Empire for entrepreneurs. Moreover, I received the Spirit of Entrepreneurship scholarship twice during my undergrad at California State University. It was one of the reasons why I even chose Entrepreneurial Management as a major in the first place. As an entrepreneurial student, I used to volunteer to set up the event hall to get a ticket to the ceremony at the Riverside Convention Center. Of course, I could have bought myself a ticket, but why do so when I could be involved in the setup? The ceremony night came, and I got all dressed up as people do for red carpet events. While I didn't win the award, simply being nominated meant more to me than the plaque itself. It was such an incredible honor that my classmates and professors on campus congratulated me for months, weeks, and days leading up to the event. God had shown me that I was a winner and that my friends were all the validation I needed. For the rest of the night and for days to follow, I praised God for that unforgettable experience. Being honored on so many levels only confirmed that I was on the right path to success. Unbeknownst to many, I was still struggling overcoming challenges and trying to avoid burnout.

One of the most pressing concerns with my business was accounting. I needed to find an accountant, a good one that I could trust. As entrepreneurs, we wear so many hats that we sometimes don't know when to stop and ask for help. One night on Facebook I was going through the friends I had recently accepted friendship requests from and came across a guy named Joe. I looked through his profile and saw that he also had graduated from Cal State San Bernardino and he had an accounting firm. Then I noticed we had Ray as a friend in common, which made me give him the benefit of the doubt. If he was friends with Ray, he had to be good people, right? I didn't want to trust just anyone with my QuickBooks, and my business was also operating in the red. I didn't want anyone in my business if they could not help me. I was very picky.

I thought about it and then reached out to Joe on October 29, 2019. It was a big deal for me to reach out to someone about finances—that's why I remember the date. But I knew at the rate I was going, without a professional in accounting, it could have been disastrous or, God forbid, close down my business. So, I decided it was time to stop being scared of what could go wrong if I brought in someone to see the mess I had made of my QuickBooks and start getting excited about everything that could go right.

I typed my direct message: "You don't know me, but we have a friend in common that recently passed away, and I'm thinking that since you were such good friends, I'm hoping you can help me with my accounting."

He responded right away.

"I sent you a friend request, and you accepted it but never said anything. The way you treated Ray, the way he would smile and enjoy himself when he was with you, just made me want to become friends with you."

Until that moment I had completely forgotten I had befriended him on Facebook! I told him I needed his help.

"With what?" he asked.

"My books are not so good. I need your help to guide me, to make my business survive."

He said, "Okay. When can we meet so I can look at your books?"

We decided to meet at Cal State San Bernardino on November 17—two weeks later. He asked for my credit score. I said it was horrible (around 500). His simple reaction, "Okay," was something.

I then gave him access to my QuickBooks account. Again, the same reaction, "Okay!"

"Don't judge me, first of all," I said. "Second of all, I've been doing it all by myself. I don't have money. I'm just hanging on so my business can make it," I explained to him. "I am doing this by myself and am a single mom of two girls. And I am a recent divorcee because my ex-husband did not want to be married to an ex-stripper. It's taboo in my culture to do that type of dancing."

Joe is from Palestine, and he could relate to such cultural issues. However, his response about my ex-husband was so matter of fact. "Fuck him. That's his loss," he said. *My sentiments exactly*, I thought to myself.

I knew then Joe was the person to help me with my business. I told him I didn't have any money, as he could see from the presented documents, but I would do my best to pay him a certain amount. So we understood that he would do my books for a cost I could afford. He then visited my website and told me I needed to update my website professionally. Again, because I had little money when I started my business, I paid a guy whom someone referred to me to design the site for $400. I never really put too much effort into it. It was just something for customers to visit. Joe told me I needed to upgrade my site now if I wanted customers to take my business seriously. He told me about his brother, Tarek, a web designer. Joe and his brother are partners in a marketing company. At first, I wondered if Joe wanted to help me or help himself. I thought him bringing in his brother was a way of him getting more money out of me. Again, I was so low on funds that everything was suspicious. Plus, I had not trusted anyone else for a long time, so I scrutinized everything he did with a fine-tooth comb.

When Tarek gave me the price to update my website, I said, "This is ridiculous." It was a huge investment for a struggling entrepreneur. Nevertheless, I complied. I agreed to make a deposit and payment arrangements, and he started working on my website in November 2019. The results were mind-blowing when he completed my website in late December 2019. I never imagined my website could look so good and be so easy to navigate. The website's relaunch was a hit. The customer feedback was all good. They told me the website was beautiful—some even wanted Tarek's contact information for their websites. Once I saw my customer base growing due to the website upgrade, I started to believe more in Joe's intention to grow my business and build my empire. His idea of upgrading the website was brilliant. That was when I trusted him a little bit more.

Then, Joe began to clean my QuickBooks. I used the desktop QuickBooks for the first two years of the business and had been doing a messy accounting job. I was not fond of accounting in school; I only studied it because it was one of the required classes for my degree. But I used what I learned and applied it to my business. Joe used the online QuickBooks version and made everything look understandable and accessible, so I could easily understand my business numbers.

I must confess. I doubted Joe because I saw him as a money-hungry guy with outrageous fees. But good accounting was needed if I wanted the company to grow. Joe was so money-driven that I started telling him money is not everything. He responded that money is not everything, but money is needed to live a comfortable life.

He understood I wanted to build wealth and a legacy for my children, but I won't sell my soul. My services come at a premium price, and that is because my customers understand the value and benefits of the products I use during services. Once Joe understood my beliefs and values, he proved he could guide me to take my business to the next level. I began listening to more of his suggestions for the company. Some I put into practice, while others I attempted but they didn't work. During this back-and-forth with Joe, a friendship started to evolve. I now consider him to be an excellent friend. I genuinely believe Joe was God-sent because I prayed for God to send me someone to help me handle my business and personal finances. I celebrate our friendship every chance I get by praying for his business and mine.

I ask him for advice on investing and even shopping. When I go shoe shopping (he knows how much I love shoes!) or even inventory for the salon, before buying something outrageous, I hear him in my head: "You have a goal—to build your empire. The shoes can wait." I am laughing as I write this part.

Before Joe came into the picture, I always bought things for the business. But, he explained, "You'll never see a profit if you keep buying. So before buying more, you must wait until you're almost out of the product. You don't want products sitting on the self."

I also seek his advice for other things, such as saving for a down payment to buy my house. Over the years, I had destroyed my credit, and creditors were hunting me down. With Joe's advice, I have been able to rebuild my FICO score to purchase a home.

He is such a significant part of my life. I would freak out when I didn't hear from him for a week and vice versa. Then, in May 2020, he was hospitalized with pancreatitis and was unable to respond to my text messages. I started panicking. He always responded to my text messages no matter the time of the day. He finally answered and told me he was at the hospital and would be there for weeks. So, of course, I went into panic mode. Then I turned to God because as far as I knew, God put Joe into my life through our mutual friendship with Ray.

"Heavenly Father, you brought this Joe into my life to help me with my business, and now here he is in a hospital, and this is COVID time. Father, I ask you to cover him with the blood of your son, Jesus Christ, and bring him out of the hospital to his family and clients that need and want his services. Please heal and take care of him for all those his life touches. In Jesus' name, Amen."

I don't take my friendships lightly. I stay loyal to my friends or anyone with good intentions for my well-being. That's why you can count my friends, and I mean my honest friends, on one hand. I lost two of my good friends in 2019. I didn't want to experience the loss of another one. When Joe got released from the hospital, we talked about taking care of himself and his health. Knowing he was home with his family gave me peace of mind. He was on the road to recovery, and I knew I wouldn't be looking for his replacement soon. Selfish of me to think of not losing an accountant? Maybe. But, he is more than just an accountant to me; he is a friend and supporter. In addition to my parents and daughters, he supports my vision for my business wholeheartedly. Having Joe has been a blessing in my life. I see endless possibilities in growing my company.

Just My Tu Sense
(Lesson Learned)

———•••◆•••———

Education is important for running a business but so is determination and sheer grit. In the United States, it's important to have a good credit score; don't screw up your credit.

PART 7
NEVADA

Chapter 26
You're Going to Vegas!

"You can be scared. You can be nervous. You can be uncertain. Show up anyways - that's how you will succeed."

- ANONYMOUS

Everything I had envisioned for Tu Organics LLC was starting to manifest. I was now teaching regularly at Riverside Community College and creating jobs with paid employees and independent contractors. It felt good! I saw growth because when Joe and I went over the numbers every month, the financials showed the salon had begun operating in the green. Although there was no big profit, I paid all the bills on time. It was exciting to see the possibilities and potential for expansion.

In January 2020, I thought *this was a new beginning.* I was finally reaching my goal in revenue. Joe and I were outlining a plan for the year and how to execute it. But, you know the saying, "While you are planning, God is laughing?" Well, in March 2020, the COVID-19 pandemic hit.

Governor Gavin Newsom shut everything down. Businesses. Schools. Offices. Everything. The governor placed a stay-at-home order to "flatten the curve" for two weeks. It wasn't only in California; the entire world shut down. My independent contractors left, and I also let my employees go and told them they could return when we reopened. I accepted the shutdown as perhaps a sign I needed to slow down and take a break. I had been going for four years straight, nonstop like a well-oiled machine. I ate, slept, and drank Tu Organics Salon and Spa. I needed and wanted to spend time with my seven-year-old and also relax. It was unfortunate that it took the COVID-19 shutdown to do so. Ophelia loved having me with her 24/7. I loved and enjoyed every minute as well.

As I waited for the shutdown to end, I asked God, myself, and Joe: "Now what?"

"What do you mean 'now what'?" Joe asked. "Do some YouTube videos. Do online teachings."

So I started a YouTube channel and uploaded videos on it. But, unfortunately, it is not easy to have people subscribe to a YouTube channel, making it difficult to stay motivated. Meanwhile I faced another challenge or roadblock. Someone reported me to the city of Rancho Cucamonga, saying I was working inside my salon during the shutdown. A gentleman showed up at my salon while I was recording a video to warn me and tell me to go home until we were allowed to reopen, rumored to be around mid-May. A lack of subscribers and then someone reporting me made me tired and unmotivated to continue with the YouTube videos. I stopped doing them. However, Joe was a nag that was not going away. He kept pushing me. Every conversation we had was about me getting up and doing something. Anyone who has worked with Joe knows he is the most stubborn man. We kept at it, going back and forth. It was nonstop.

Because of his industry, he stayed watching the news, which did not interest me. I was not fueling myself with negative energy, which in my opinion, is what the news gives. So I stay away from the news channels, especially as they continued to report about the many people dying from COVID. Joe, however, learned and shared information about applying for the SBA Economic Injury Disaster Loan and unemployment.

"But I don't think I qualify," I said

"Apply! It won't hurt." So I did and waited.

My independent contractors then let me know they could not continue paying their booth rents. I told them I understood because it was unfair, and they appreciated me. The following day, in early May, I received an email from Chase Bank, alerting me of a deposit made to my business account. It was from the Economic Injury Disaster program. It was enough to cover my rent for a month, which I very much appreciated because the building management was still sending rent invoices. I was behind for both April and May, though the building management had reached out to me with a payment plan and I took her up on the offer. I kept my cool and kept my Bible close to my heart while Joe was freaking out for me and reminding me every chance he got by saying things like, "I know you're not going to sit around and let your business fail."

To me, God was working on my behalf. All I had to do was have faith. In mid-May, I was lying in bed with Ophelia watching Netflix, like everyone else in America because there was nothing else to do, when I received an email from the Small Business Administration. I had been pre-approved for an SBA loan for an amount that I could not believe was possible for me. I could not control my excitement. I immediately forwarded the email to Joe, who of course did all the calculations. It was all God's doing!

COVID-19 was both a blessing and a curse in my life, but more of a gift. After signing and sending all the required documents, SBA deposited the money into my business account during the last week of May. I arranged for Chase Bank to mail all back and current rent payments to the salon building management to bring my balance to zero.

I then called ACCION and paid my business loan in full. I also paid back the loan I had taken from my parents. All the bills were up to date. and there was still money left to run my business once we reopened. I was completing my last quarter as an MBA student at Cal State San Bernardino and shared the fantastic news with my classmates and one of my professors, Bill Donohoo. Everyone was excited for me, especially Bill because he had a front-row seat throughout my start-up journey. He had been a mentor to me while at CSUSB. He helped with my financial projects for the business plan. He attended my grand opening and still supports my business by getting his hair cut from me. For a class project, we expanded my salon idea to Las Vegas and created an employee handbook for Tu Organics LLC.

In June 2020, California allowed hair salons (among other places) to reopen. I had to work outside, however. I would make some appointments to work outside, but we went inside when the weather got too hot because it was in the middle of summer. I scheduled private appointments for clients, which was harmless because the clients and I had the salon to ourselves. My employees stayed at home. I was not ready for them to return to work; I was not sure if we would get shut down again. My independent contractors decided to stay at home because they were older and in the high-risk group for contracting the COVID-19 virus. When a new surge of COVID cases started again, hair salons were shut down again in California in July 2020.

This time, Joe told me: "You're going to Vegas."

"I'm not going to Vegas."

"Don't you see? Vegas is open."

"So?"

"Get your Nevada license and go to Vegas."

"Joe, I am not going to Vegas! You know I have a seven-year-old daughter," I pushed back. "I'm not leaving my Ophelia."

"You'll figure it out. You're going to get it done. Because if you keep paying the salon rent bills with the money you received as a loan from the SBA and not generating income, you will soon run out of funds."

"Joe, do you understand what you are asking me to do?"

"I know what I am asking you to do if you want your business to survive COVID-19. You can use your parents' empty house in Vegas and look for a salon suite. Plus, you can drive back and forth from California and Vegas. It's only a three-and-a-half-hour drive," he said.

"I don't want to do that!"

"If you don't do that, your business is going to go down the drain," he said. "You don't know when you're going to open up again for business."

At the time, I was collecting unemployment, which I never thought was possible because I was a business owner. But I also worked for RCC as a cosmetology instructor. So I gave in and decided to try Joe's way. I went to the Nevada State Board of Cosmetology website and applied for a reciprocity license. I paid the application fee and a week later, I set up an appointment for an exam via Zoom. The exam was twenty-five questions long related to Nevada rules and regulations on cosmetology. I studied, and on the day of the exam, I started it at 9:00 a.m. and finished by 9:15 a.m. The lady was so surprised by how quickly I finished. But, of course, "I'm also a cosmetology instructor!" I told her.

Congratulations, your license will arrive in two weeks.

By late July 2020, I was looking for a location to work in Nevada. I couldn't believe it! This guy (Joe) got me to go to another state, and I don't know how I was going to make it happen. But it was happening—and fast!

I received my cosmetology license on August 6. It had been an exhilarating experience—from the day I started the whole process to the day I received my license. After that, I posted on social media:

"Call me crazy. Tu Organics Salon and Spa is going to Las Vegas."

CHAPTER 27
TU IN NEVADA

"Before tasting success, you are likely to face many setbacks and failures. But the trick is to never let go of your enthusiasm, perseverance, and positive attitude."

- JOSEPH PARKER

Once I got to Nevada, I started driving around, looking for the perfect location. I went to the area around the Allegiant Stadium and said, "No, that's not a good location for my salon." On the second day, I went to Henderson. Not for me. My next stop was Summerlin. It was the right location for Tu Organics Salon and Spa. I wrote down the names of salon suites to call once I returned to California. I found one inside the Body Spa Salon, which I would have to share with a gentleman doing body sculpting. A month later, I set up shop.

By August 9, 2020, I had my salon suite set up and was ready for my first clients on August 10. Finally, Tu Organics Salon and Spa's second location was a reality! My first client was one of my former clients from California. When she moved to Nevada, she would return to California and get her haircuts with me. She always asked when I would come to Vegas. She was so happy that I opened this new location.

However, I learned the gentleman I was sharing the space with was a scammer. After seeing a few red flags, my intuition told me to get out. When you get that feeling in your stomach that does not feel right, your intuition is talking to you and you better listen. I told that man that our agreement would not work, and I wanted out of our deal. About six months after getting out of our contract, the manager at the Las Vegas building where I had shared a space with that guy texted me his mugshot. Apparently, Nevada police arrested him for operating without a license and child molestation. Whew! God is always looking out for me. I give Him the glory.

Anyway, I stayed in the same building but had my own hairstyling station for Tu Organics Salon. I officially started in my space in late September. The business was challenging and slow to grow. I began to feel disappointed and questioned my decision.

I would go off on Joe saying, "This is all your fault! If I don't make it, I swear, Joe, our friendship and business dealings, as we know it, will come to an end!"

He would reassure me, saying, "You have just arrived and can't expect overnight success. Try advertising."

I used Groupon to advertise and it started to bring in customers. But, Groupon customers are not loyal; they only care for deals. Slowly, Summerlin began to take on a life of its own, and so did my salon. I now travel to Nevada once a month and work nonstop, sometimes to the point of feeling burnout. But, I keep motivating myself by thinking positive thoughts and what the result will be one day.

Even with the challenge of building a client base, the Nevada start-up journey was much more comfortable than the California location. It might be because I had done it before. In addition, the experience was less stressful, perhaps because I am only renting a salon chair instead of having a traditional brick-and-mortar location. But stay tuned. A brick-and-mortar building is coming in the very near future.

Epilogue

When I got on that first stage as an exotic dancer, I was a terrified young lady, shaking in my thigh high boots. Today, I am a strong, confident woman, standing with my head held high (and still wearing stillettos because I love heels). I'm no longer a stripper trying to survive, but a professor of cosmetology and business owner who has attained a level of success that I am super proud of.

I used to be embarrassed about my past. Remember I was scared that my family in Africa would find out? Well they did. And if I would have gone back to Sierra Leone while I was living that lifestyle, I would certainly be outcasted. But my past doesn't embarrass me. Being an exotic dancer and experiencing all the pitfalls has made me what I am today. Like Ruby Bridges said, "I now know that experience comes to us for a purpose, and if we follow that guidance of the spirit within us, we will probably find that the purpose is a good one."

I now know that my Heavenly Father wanted me to turn my trials into triumphs and my pain into purpose. I'm sure he wants me to inspire and encourage others in a similar place to where I was in my past. That's my purpose.

With all my struggles and woes, I had three visits with a therapist, and that was to address my marital problems at the time. For me, turning to the Bible and inviting God to comfort and protect me when I felt overwhelmed or insecure was my therapy. Spending time in nature, thanking my Creator for choosing to go through life with me, and knowing He is always with me no matter what I face was what I needed to heal. I have forgiven all the men for what they did to me, and I have forgiven myself for the role I played in what happened. I took responsibility for the decision I made and for my part in all of it. I genuinely believe I wouldn't be where I am today if I had held onto all that grudges and hate over the years.

Bobby apologized and asked for my forgiveness, and I forgave him. He is now happily married. Solo calls me now and then and has also asked for forgiveness. Tutu and I have had our ups and downs over the years, like every mother and daughter relationship. Although I was absent or out hustling and my mom pretty much raised her, we still have a solid relationship. I'm so proud of the woman she's becoming, on her way to being a graduate of Cal State herself, like me. I forgave him. Max is still in my life because we share custody of Ophelia. He still thinks it was all my fault. But I pray for him; I pray for all of them. I think that's why God opened up my life. Forgiveness was the biggest thing that helped me through all my trials and tribulations—that and prayers. I have gone from living paycheck to paycheck and relying on payday loans to living quite comfortably being an entrepreneur, a professor, and a businesswoman. I knew education would change everything for me. And it did.

My journey so far has been filled with several people. Some of them were toxic and led me on a downward path. I also have enjoyed the strong support of others, including my mom, who uplifted me and helped me become the success I am today. God has put me on this path to help others find their way, but He wanted me to find my way first and to appreciate myself for who I am. My mind, body, and soul have all healed from all the bad experiences in my life. I have an excellent vision for the future.

As for Tu Organics Salon and Spa, I have a lot of joy about the business and am looking forward to what the future holds. My biggest challenge over the years has been finding reliable employees. But does that mean I am going to throw in the towel? Not as long as I have my primary investor, God. He kept my salon doors open during a pandemic when others closed shop; I faced eviction during my first two years of operations. Employees have come and gone, yet my doors are open. All I can say is with God, anything is possible.

My hope for you is to find or bring God closer to you. Love your family no matter what. And learn to forgive others for you to be blessed abundantly. Find peace and joy in living your true self. Here's Tu YOUR Success!

My daughters Tutu and Ophelia

Thank God

God, I love you! You are worthy of all my praise, honor, and adoration! You heal the broken and bind up the hurting people's wounds. Your light casts out the darkness, and nothing can overcome Your Power. You are good, and Your mercy continues forever. So today, I want to focus on who You are and thank You for all You've helped me overcome. In Jesus' name, Amen.

Tu Success! A Journey from Pain To Purpose Book Resources:

- It's Your Time (IYT) Training Series - https://www.iewbc.org/
- Inland Empire Women's Business Center
- School of Entrepreneurship Program - https://www.entre.csusb.edu/
- College of Business and Public Administration at Cal State San Bernardino
- Accion of San Diego - https://www.accion.org/
- Small Business Micro Loan
- Community Action Partnership https://capriverside.org/
- A matched savings incentive program for citizens of Riverside County who qualify
- Select a domain name w/professional email (check on Google.com first) http://www.top10webhosting.com/top-web-hosting/
- Choose a legal structure (i.e. Sole Prop., Partnership, Corporation (S, C, or LLC) http://www.sos.ca.gov/business/be/starting-a-business-types.htm
- Fictitious Business Name – (and publish newspaper):
- https://www.asrclkrec.com/Clerk/FictitiousBusinessNames.aspx

- Open a bank account for the business
- Federal Employer ID Number (AKA EIN) https://www.irs.gov (or just Google: "How to get a Federal EIN number
- Seller's Permit (if you are selling a product/something tangible) - http://www.boe.ca.gov
- Business License – City Hall of your city
- Miscellaneous Licenses and Permits (depending on industry) www.calgold.ca.gov or http://ca.gov/DoingBusiness
- Insurance
- Bookkeeper/CPA (familiar with your industry)
- Attorney or Legal Protection/Advice
- Begin networking – research chambers and groups
- Join a club or professional organization in your industry
- Don't forget social media – Facebook, Twitter, Instagram, etc.... but use only what you will be consistent with; 1,000 Twitter followers won't help if you tweet once a year!
- Bankruptcy - https://www.cacb.uscourts.gov/court-locations/riverside

Acknowledgements

My deepest gratitude to Thierry Brusselle for your educational contributions to my life while I was your student at Chaffey College. I will forever be grateful for your impact on my success.

My extended gratitude to William G. Donohoo for your mentorship as my professor at California State University in San Bernardino and as my client at Tu Organics Salon and Spa. Thank you for believing in me so much that you contributed your time to the foreword of this book.

Words cannot begin to explain my gratitude to Tina Ramos-Ingold. You helped make this book come alive by contributing your time when I was caring for so many other things.

My heartfelt gratitude to my accountant and friend, Joe Nazzal, for being patient and fully committing your time to the growth of my business. Your encouragement, friendship, and support have meant so much to me.

A special thank you to my friend Daniel Riggs for always making your home available to me for my little gateways and for bringing out my playful and truthful side. Also, I appreciate Maritza Gomez for your selflessness and always being ready to share resources with women.

I am forever grateful to Michelle Skiljan for seeing how powerful my story is and motivating me to bring it to light. Thank you for being so committed to my success.

My deepest and sincere gratitude to Dr. Michael Stull, the Director and Professor at the California State University San Bernardino School of Entrepreneurship, for the tremendous role the school's scholarship played in my higher education and for the proud display of a 3' by 4' picture of me in the main seminar class.

Thank you to Ernie Silvers for providing resources to display my speaking abilities and for your encouragement.

I greatly appreciate Mary Walker for teaching me so much and igniting the light by showing me that I am worth so much. Mary took me under her wing and treated me like a daughter. She has been a mentor, a friend, and an advisor. Her encouragement helped me stay focused on my educational goals, and her guidance helped me blossom into the phenomenal woman I am today.

A magnitude of gratitude to my editor Joan Stanford; for helping me dig deep into my soul and be as vulnerable as can be and develop a book that I am genuinely proud to share with the world. Joan, you were the first to know that I intended to write a book, and we talked about it in 2016. You were there for the grand opening of my business, and here we are, the manifestation of my book, six years later.

My sister, Susan Mogren, thank you for never judging me and for loving and accepting me for who I am. You are dear to my heart. Although we've had our differences in the past, Sarah and Ella, you will always be my blood sisters, and I love you both.

Tutu and Ophelia, I cannot imagine my life without you. You are the reasons why I breathe. Your love has made my world. I pray that you both always stand up for yourselves and never remain silent. I pray that God gives you wisdom, guides your parts, and gives you the lives your heart's desire.

To my amazing supporters of Tu Success! Brent Mickey, Alexandra Samuel-Sturgess, Andrew Mendez, Beverly Landry, Heidi Case, Deborah Allen, Juhi Singh, Kevin Zydzik, Marivic Burger, Keyana Holloway, Kimesha Malone, Sonja Hubley, Stella Ndahura, Maritza Gómez and Susan Mogren for being the first to pre-order my memoir. Your immediate action of pre-ordering my book showed me that you all meant what you said. Thank you.

Finally, I thank clients like Ms. Shirlee Watson, Ms. Luella Hairston, Olga Javier, and countless others who have supported my business. Tu Organics Salon and Spa won't be here six years later without your loyalty. I greatly appreciate you all.